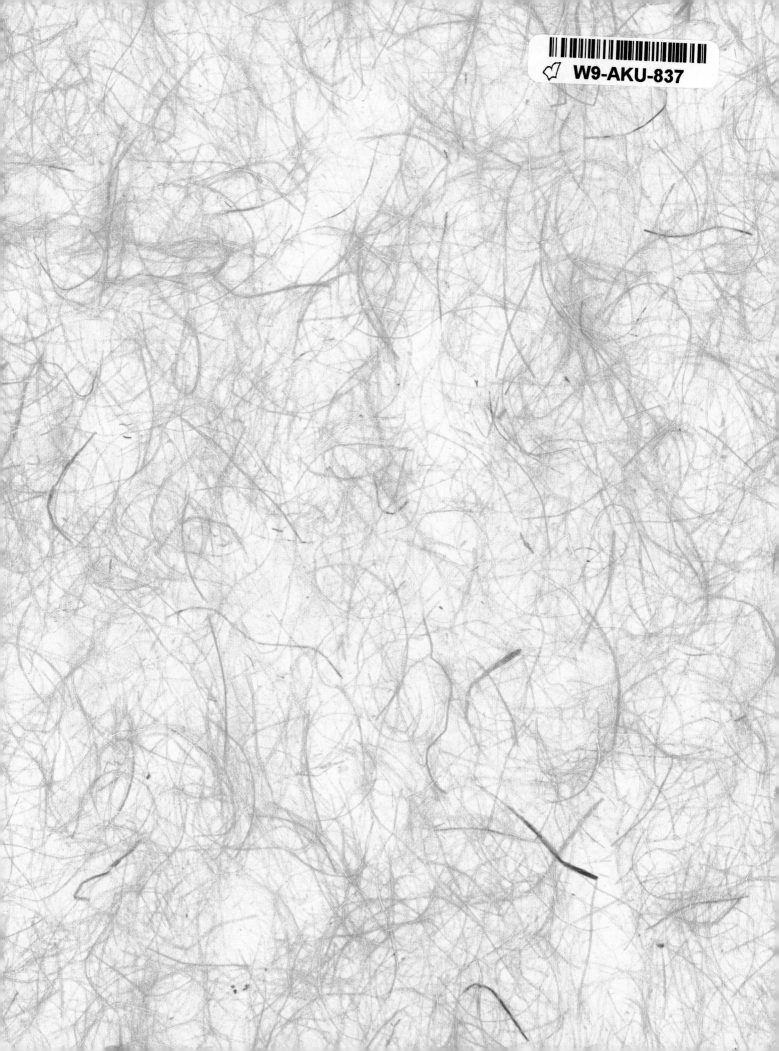

Victorian Gardens

Caroline Holmes

Schiffer Publishing Ltd

4880 Lower Valley Road, Atglen, PA 19310, USA

Dedication

To Will for his unerring eye for form and style not forgetting his stalwart attitude that ensures a project is completed

A flower filled stone crater in the Victorian gardens at Calke Abbey.

Library of Congress Cataloging-in-Publication Data

Holmes, Caroline.
    Victorian gardens / by Caroline Holmes.
       p. cm.
    Includes bibliographical references and index.
    ISBN 0-7643-1889-6
1. Gardens, Victorian--England--History. I. Title.
SB458.7 .H66 2005
716'.0942--dc21

2003010898

Designed by "Ellen J. (Sue) Taltoan
Type set in Shelly Alegro BT/Dutch801 Rm BT

ISBN: 0-7643-1889-6
Printed in China

Published by Schiffer Publishing Ltd.
4880 Lower Valley Road
Atglen, PA 19310
Phone: (610) 593-1777; Fax: (610) 593-2002
E-mail: Info@schifferbooks.com
Please visit our web site catalog at www.schifferbooks.com
We are always looking for people to write books on new and related subjects. If you have an idea for a book, please contact us at the above address.

This book may be purchased from the publisher.
Include $3.95 for shipping.
Please try your bookstore first.
You may write for a free catalog.

In Europe, Schiffer books are distributed by
Bushwood Books
6 Marksbury Avenue
Kew Gardens
Surrey TW9 4JF England
Phone: 44 (0) 20 8392 8585
Fax: 44 (0) 20 8392 9876
E-mail: info@bushwoodbooks.co.uk
Free postage in the UK. Europe: air mail at cost.

Contents

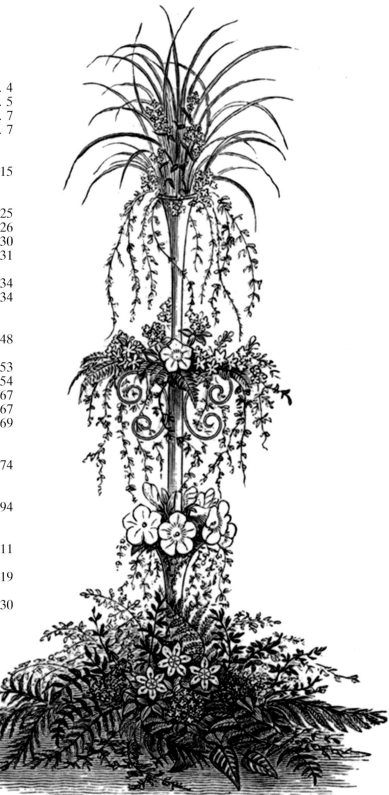

"Arrangement of tubular flowers" as a magnificent centerpiece for house or garden.

Fig. 784.—Arrangement of Tubular Flowers.

Acknowledgments

I have worked on and around Victorian gardens for many years. My initial research was sparked by the Museum of Garden History for whom I ran the Victorian Garden Study Days for many years. The Museum's enthusiastic support through, initially, Rosemary Nicholson, and now Anne Jennings and Phillip Norman has been and is great. Similarly, Bob Sherman, Susan Turner, and Katie Butler at HDRA, Yalding, for so brilliantly interpreting and creating the Victorian Artisan's Garden. For this book, an enormous thank you to Twigs Way for enabling me to transfer so many original illustrations from my books onto disk not to mention her unfailing support and enthusiasm in all our work. Equally, Erica Hunningher for her finishing touches and Tina Skinner for narrowing the borders. Last but not least my husband, David, bookfinder general.

Introduction

Whether you live in a Victorian property or not, welcome to the joys of nineteenth century certainty and eclecticism. Victorian home gardeners avidly sought knowledge in a panoply of gardening books and magazines, many of which are still readily available. They tend to be too detailed for modern tastes but you can still enjoy the sentiment and enthusiasm if not the practicalities. A typical example is Sam Beeton's introduction for Victorian amateur gardeners written in the 1860s:

When a man becomes the possessor of a garden, whether as owner or tenant, it will be found that there are three conditions in one or the other of which it must of necessity be. Thus, firstly, it may be new ground utterly innocent of form and arrangement which has to be brought into a fit state for the culture of flowers, vegetables, and fruits; secondly, it may be a garden which is in cultivation and ready to hand throughout - a garden which has been well worked, well kept, and well stocked, and therefore a garden in its prime; or, thirdly, it may be an old garden which requires renovating and bringing once more into proper form and capability of yielding remunerative crops.

Victoria came to the British throne in 1837 (The Victorian Artisan's Garden, HDRA, Kent).

Before Queen Victoria came to the throne in 1837, smaller gardens in towns and villages were tended for pleasure and profit but her reign witnessed gardening grow as a home leisure pursuit. Victoria reigned for nearly sixty-four years and the word Victorian for this period is a term used and recognized in many parts of the world.

Joseph Paxton was described by his contemporary Samuel Smiles as *"a man who cultivated opportunities – a laborious, painstaking man, whose life had been a life of labour, of diligent self-improvement of assiduous cultivation of knowledge."* Paxton had started work as his brother's assistant at Battlesden Park, Bedfordshire and then worked for the Duke of Somerset. By the age of twenty-three he was foreman of the arboretum at the Horticultural Society's Chiswick gardens which was on land leased from the Duke of Devonshire. The Duke then appointed Paxton superintendent of his gardens at Chatsworth in Derbyshire. Paxton constructed the Great Conservatory or Stove at Chatsworth between 1836 and 1840 in collaboration with Decimus Burton; it was fashioned as a compromise between the curvilinear style and the more popular ridge and furrow design.

In 1841 Paxton helped to establish the magazine, *The Gardener's Chronicle*, which recorded all the latest plant introductions and profiled important Victorian gardens. It was edited by John Lindley of the Horticultural Society at Chiswick and was first published in the same year that the Royal Botanical Gardens at Kew were opened to the public for the first time. In 1845 the tax on glass was repealed and through the columns of *The Gardener's Chronicle* Paxton marketed cheaper, modular greenhouses. They were assembled by means of timber framed sashes containing a number of glazed lights in standard lengths – ideally suited to the small Victorian garden. Variations provided lean-to or span-roofed houses, both easily constructed with hinged ventilation panels between each pair of sashes.

On May Day 1851 Queen Victoria opened the Great Exhibition Building designed by Paxton which *Punch* magazine nicknamed the Crystal Palace. Before the exhibition closed on 15th October, Victoria had visited thirty-four times and 6,200,000 visitors from all over the world had also come to admire the latest in Victorian technology from steam engines to bedding plants. The Exhibition was described as a *triumph of art and horticultural skill over nature*, a triumph to be emulated throughout the Empire. Paxton became Member of Parliament for Coventry and initiated the designing and landscaping of city parks and cemeteries. Great Exhibitions in similar style were held in Paris in 1889 and 1900 and in 1892 the Columbian Exhibition was held in Chicago.

In the States, in the 1842 preface to *Cottage Residences,* Andrew Downing wrote:

But I am still more anxious to inspire in the minds of my readers and countrymen more lively perceptions of the BEAUTIFUL in everything that relates to our houses and grounds. I wish to awaken a quicker sense of the grace, the elegance, or the picturesqueness of fine forms that are capable of being produced in these by Rural Architecture and Landscape Gardening – a sense (that) *will not only refine and elevate the mind, but pour into it new and infinite resources of delight.*

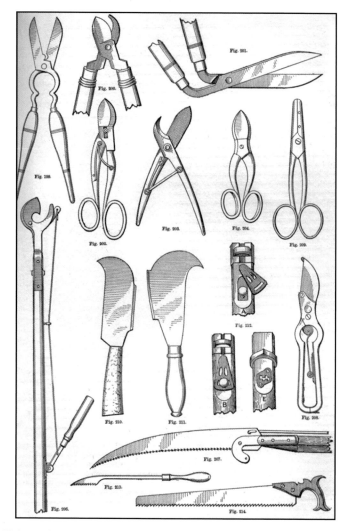

Knives of various kinds are required in gardens, for pruning, budding, grafting, and other purposes advised Thompson's *Gardeners Assistant.* Illustrated are: 199 Hedge, 200 Lopping, 201 Grass-edging, and 202, 203, 204 Pruning Shears; 205 Standard Tree-pruner, 208 Secateur, 209 Flower Gatherer, 210, 211 Bill-hook and 212 scythe-snaths which were used for attaching the blade to the shaft.

The Victorians gardened in a variety of styles: the Italianate style was very popular at the beginning of Victoria's reign with its sense of order and proportion, brightly colored by the newly introduced tender bedding plants. William Andrews Nesfield and Charles Barry designed dramatic terraces and gardens which reintroduced geometric formality around many of the grand houses in Britain. Many urban and suburban gardens tried to echo this style with bright, formal, seasonal bedding providing visual treats throughout the garden.

On the other hand, English poet, artist, craftsman, decorator, and social reformer, William Morris was a prime mover in the sociological and aesthetic aims of the Arts and Crafts Movement. In simple terms they were inspired by medieval craftsmanship when gardens, like buildings and furnishings, were crafted out of local materials growing hardy and native plants. Philip Webb designed and built the Red House, Bexley Heath for Morris and his wife Jane, whose rose trellis inspired one of the first fabrics produced by his company, Morris, Marshal, Faulkner & Co. In turn I replicated that design for the Victorian Artisan's Garden for HDRA – the Organic Organization at Yalding in Kent.

These garden sentiments and the dislike of over-artificiality in flowers was shared by William Robinson who founded *The Garden* magazine in 1871. Robinson encouraged the movement towards natural plantings complemented by hardy American introductions; he traveled regularly to France and North America. His garden at Gravetye Manor in Sussex was filled with drifts of hardy and native trees, shrubs, and flowers. Indefatigable, he kept a twenty year diary of his planting successes and failures at Gravetye, replacing tens of thousands of bulbs eaten by rabbits until he had springtime drifts under his trees (a style emulated today in parks and gardens). His *The English Flower Garden*, still in print, is just as valuable today especially if you revel in dogmatic certainty. Alfred Parsons painted in the gardens at Gravetye as well as illustrating for Robinson. Robinson's books and craftsman-like approach appealed to Pre-Raphaelite and Arts and Crafts followers alike, and his advocacy of water lilies and clematis is recognized in varieties named for him and his head gardener, Ernest Markham.

The large selection of gardening magazines and encyclopedias, the founding of Horticultural Societies and Garden Clubs as well as excellent nurseries enabled the small Victorian garden to display a diversity of styles and plants. A walk through such gardens provided *"incidents"* or points of interest worthy of closer scrutiny and discussion. Enthusiasm and a pleasure in your own surroundings are the primary ingredients for cultivating a sense of the Victorian past on your plot.

The following numbered plan appeared in Beeton's *Shilling Gardening Book* written by Sam Beeton, husband and publisher of Mrs. Isabella Beeton of Household Management fame. He writes that where it can be so arranged the garden should be an oblong square. In this plan the dimensions are three hundred feet by two hundred ten feet, the arrow on the house points north. The driveway dominates the west boundary, the south and east have walls or buildings and finally, a deep shrubbery lines the north surrounded by a low brick wall with green iron railings. All the paths are curving providing walks that introduce and hide *"incidents"* within the garden.

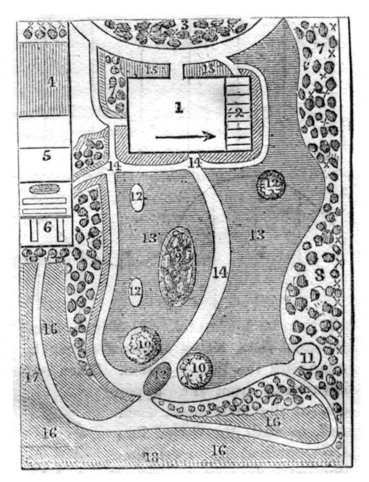

Beeton's "A Convenient Villa Garden." 1. The villa or house, the arrow is pointing north; 2. The conservatory; 3. A clump of trees and shrubs fronting the main entrance which also provide privacy from the road; 4. Coach house and stables; 5. Tool house; 6. Manure and frame yard situated near the stables, few today will have horses in their stables so this would be the place for compost heaps; 7. Flower borders and shrubberies that shelter and disguise; 8. Ferns and American plants are afforded shade by the surrounding beds; 9. Rose clumps; 10. Circular beds (approximately twenty-five feet diameter); 11. Arbor-note that it is tucked out of sight from the house and main paths nestling in the shrubs; 12. Flower beds-the Victorian equivalent to modern island beds but planted with seasonal flowers and foliage (see *The Plantation Garden* later); 13. Lawn; 14. Paths; 15. Beds for placing out flowers in pots;16. Kitchen gardens-extensive for modern tastes; 17. Peach wall (and vineries, forcing houses, and orchard houses); 18. East facing wall for plums, cherries, and pears.

1. The villa has a good garden door. Make the most of a garden door or French windows with a short flight of steps, pots arranged around the door, or wall shrubs and climbers.

2. The conservatory is as valuable today as then, cleverly warming the north side of the house and enjoying early morning sun.

A Victorian conservatory, then as now, provides "a more propitious clime," in Beeton's plan cleverly warming the north side of the house. *The Plantation Garden, Norwich.*

3. A clump of trees and shrubs fronting the main entrance provides privacy from the road; underplant with seasonal bulbs.

4. Coach house and stables, a Victorian luxury, today probably either converted and sold off or housing the car. The water feature illustrated on page 128 is actually attached to the back of the owner's garage.

5. Tool house. There has been a revival in hand made and specialist tools for every garden task; store them properly and work in here when it is raining.

Large Victorian gardens had a range of sheds; on a smaller establishment the tool shed could double as a store for onions and garlic.

6. Manure and frame yard situated near the stables. Few today will have horses in their stables so this would be the place for compost heaps and cold frames.

7. Flower borders and shrubbery, preferably evergreen, shelter and disguise the manure and frame yard as well as the tool sheds. On the north boundaries, the inner edge is south facing drawing blooms and leaves towards the house and garden whilst protecting it from cold winds.

8. Ferns and American plants are afforded shade by the surrounding beds; at the time it was still widely believed in England that American plants needed boggy conditions. Beeton might well have put a small fountain in this area.

Ferns are afforded shade by the surrounding trees; Beeton might well have put a small fountain in this area. *Eshott Hall, Northumberland.*

9. Rose clumps. This oval bed is approximately fifty feet by twenty-five feet and would have featured Bourbon, China, Hybrid Perpetual, and Pillar roses. Standard roses were newly introduced and highly prized.

10. Circular beds (approximately twenty-five feet diameter) for hollyhocks, dahlias, and other free blooming plants throughout the summer and thinly planted with evergreens to take off the nakedness in winter.

STANDARD ROSES WITH VIOLAS.

Here the well-known variety, Caroline Testout, is used as a standard. This, one of the best of all Hybrid Teas, with brilliant pink flowers, was introduced by Pernet fils-Ducher, in 1890. It makes a good bush. There is a climbing form.

Standard roses offer more height and formality than bushes and opportunity for seasonal underplanting.

Decorative circular beds (approx fifteen feet diameter) of bright seasonal flowers. *The Plantation Garden, Norwich.*

11

11. Arbor. Note that it is tucked out of sight from the house and main paths nestling in the shrubs; the ideal place for a secret tryst. Andrew Downing provided his American readers with a list of twelve scented climbers for the seventy-five feet by one hundred fifty feet garden of *A Suburban Cottage for a Small Family:* six Honeysuckle, two Chinese Twining, one each Monthly Fragrant, Yellow Trumpet, Red Trumpet; one sweet scented Clematis, one Virginian Silk, one Chinese Wistaria, one climbing Boursalt Rose, and two Noisette Climbing Rose.

Two arbors: in the foreground a slatted iron seat around a six foot standard rose bush; amongst the trees, a rustic thatched shelter. *The Swiss Garden, Bedfordshire.*

The Victorians took great pride in crafted garden ornament encapsulated in the intricate delights of this arbor. *Arley Hall, Cheshire.*

12. Flower beds. The Victorian equivalent to modern island beds but planted with seasonal flowers and foliage.

13. Lawn. Well mown lawns set off the flower beds and, if troubled by moss, Beeton suggests spreading very fine coal ash over affected areas just before rain. Edwin Budding had invented the lawn mower in 1830, but most domestic lawns were still scythed. By 1842 in the United States, Andrew Downing wrote *"Frequent mowing is necessary to insure that velvet-like appearance so much admired in English lawns. To perform this operation neatly, the mower must be provided with a scythe the blade of which is very broad, and hung nearly parallel to the surface of the lawn."*

Lawn – well mown lawns set off the flower beds and, if troubled by moss, Beeton suggests spreading very fine coal ash over affected areas just before rain.

14. Paths. It is interesting to note that even the service paths from the yard through the kitchen garden are curving (see the illustration on page 111).

15. Beds for placing out flowers and/or topiary in pots. In this way the entrance of the house looks bright for all seasons.

16. Kitchen gardens. These are extensive for modern tastes but could be simply interpreted with fruits, perennial vegetables, and herbs. Seek out some heritage vegetable seed for flavor.

17. Peach wall (and vineries, forcing houses, and orchard houses). The work involved might be better used training climbing shrubs and roses as well as espalier fruits.

18. Wall for plums, cherries, and pears.

A domestic sized Peach "case" – the most important task being to keep rain off the peaches *Sunnycroft, Shropshire*.

Chapter One

Restoration – The Plantation Garden, Norwich

A guided walk around the garden Henry Trevor created, its features and plants

Henry Trevor epitomizes the industrious middle class Victorian. He was born in Wisbech, Cambridgeshire in 1819 to a retired farmer and Dissenter. It is likely that Chapel brought him to Norwich to work for the successful upholsterer and preacher Joseph Gray. In 1843 Trevor married Gray's widowed daughter and took on her three children. Of their own four subsequent children only their first, Eliza, survived.

The newlyweds lived over the shop in Post-Office Street, Norwich for seven years before moving to a "modern house" in the healthy air of the suburbs. This house overlooked an ancient chalk quarry. Trevor decided to lease this in 1855 for seventy-five years with the intention of creating *beautiful and picturesque* grounds on the three acres. In 1856 he built an austere classically styled house, aptly named "The Plantation," with a smaller dwelling for his gardener. He lived and worked on the gardens here until his death in 1897 creating a manifestation of his horticultural knowledge, religious principles, and trade prosperity. Trevor "*…believed that a man's home should be the dearest and happiest spot on earth to him,*" a quality exuded in this Victorian garden.

The Plantation Garden in spring from the Rustic Bridge. *The Plantation Garden, Norwich.*

The quarry provided a showcase in which to create a garden. The highest level dominated by the house, a middle walk tracing its route halfway along the steep sides, and finally the base decorated with textbook examples of Victorian bedding schemes. By the lower entrance was the gardener's cottage – a subtle social statement. Trevor wanted to share his magnificent garden with horticultural societies, church groups including Dissenters, Church of England, the YMCA, and other worthy causes, both by providing plants and welcoming visitors.

The gardens demonstrate two Victorian styles – Italianate and Arts and Crafts. Curiously, the word "formal" was not used to describe gardens until Reginald Blomfield coined the term in the 1890's. Until then, firstly Italian, Dutch or French, then simply Italianate style was used to describe balustraded terrace gardens with flights of steps, statuary and urns and manicured, seasonally spectacular flower beds. The Arts and Crafts movement favored vernacular materials, in this case flints, carrstone, and bricks, with native or hardy perennial planting, heavily influenced by medieval (Gothic) craftsmanship and Shakespearean romance.

The network of curving walks provided the family and visitors with a selection of interesting strolls positively crowded with incident. One enters on the upper level to the house or across the Rustic Bridge (restored in 1998) from which one gets a magnificent view up the garden to the Italian Terrace, usefully and decoratively shoring up the quarry end. In 1871 Boulton & Paul of Norwich supplied a Palm House (an octagon twenty-five feet in diameter) and attached glass Winter Garden (thirty-five feet by fifteen feet), the outlines have been turned into flowerbeds today. In this, Trevor not only raised a range of exotics and bedding plants but was also able to welcome visitors all year round. The Italian Terrace dramatically ascended by balustraded steps to where, formerly, Mrs. Henry Trevor would have taken tea in the swan decorated Summerhouse. Had Trevor read contemporary articles about the Italian gardens at the Villa Garzoni? – the terracing is very similar.

Rustic garden bridges and furniture used locally-gathered wood so that the finished product blended into the garden setting.

The extent of the garden and its *"incidents"* can be enjoyed from the Rustic Bridge culminating in the dramatic flight of steps ascending the Italian Terrace. The site of the post-1871 Palm House and Winter Garden are outlined with gravel paths; on the right, their shimmering glass and modern technology would have contrasted with the Gothic Fountain. The Fountain creates a note of history, folly, and contrast in this organized Victorian setting of neat colorful flowerbeds. The upper network of paths are concealed in the trees.

The Gothic fountain built in 1857 was the first construction or incident, offering a "prospect" from the house of a "gothic" ruin, an object for a walk to savor the delights of a grotto, a fernery, and a pool for fish and water-lilies. It combines naturally occurring flint with locally produced brickwork. Trevor wove the styles of Augustus Pugin and William Morris into the Medieval Terrace wall proudly dated 1871. His ornamental bricks were bought from the nearby Gunton Brickworks at Costessey who sold a wide range to decorate the new villas, chimneys and public buildings, as well as restored churches. Trevor created his own mix and match, mostly with the cheaper seconds that were available.

The Gothic Fountain – a folly lost in time, reminiscent of a medieval church spire providing a fountain, pool, and fernery. An ornate flint built Propagation House was behind on the right hand side.

The top is flanked by a flint wall, the center also formerly had a summer house which is being reinstated.

Below:
The balustraded top of the Medieval Wall echoes the architecture of the house. Although dated 1871, it took years to build the Arts and Crafts inspired wall with a variety of local bricks and flints. Look at the roses, thistles, artificial stonework, lintels, chimney pots, etc.

Detail of the Medieval Wall with its niches and ancient temple facades. Trevor trained diamonds of ivy across the whole wall, sadly masking his imaginative efforts.

The shadowy form of a green man in the Medieval Wall lends a surprisingly pagan note.

Beyond the Gothic Fountain is a further "ruin," in fact what was the heated propagating house swathed in ivy, today just one of its pillars survives. It measured twenty-four feet by ten feet. Trevor, the original recycler, also created a stupendous rockery out of clinker probably inspired by Shirley Hibberd's *Rustic Adornments for Homes of Taste.* Hibberd writes *"there is no better mode of constructing them than to form the foundation of brick-rubbish, and cover the whole with huge dark stones, or with those conglomerated bricks which are cast from the kilns as refuse."* Water features have been created to catch rainwater and there are pockets for dramatic showing of pot plants.

A rockery formed out of factory clinker and debris formed into channels to catch rainfall.

Below:
The recesses in the clinker rockery could be used for pots of exotics during the summer.

21

Henry Trevor searched out unusual bricks from local suppliers to decorate the walls as his visitors climbed to the top, here a vine brick.

A window on the world – Lapidary gardens were popular in France for collections of stones and architectural artifacts.

Glimpsed beyond the Gothic Fountain and Clinker Rockery rises the majestic Italian Terrace, inspired by articles in Victorian magazines on Italian gardens such as the Villa Garzoni.

The flowerbeds in the lawn today are just an echo of the labor intensive carpet bedding and mosaiculture captured in contemporary photographs. In 1890, *White's Norfolk Directory* recorded: *"The Plantation…the grounds of H. Trevor Esq., situated in a deep dell, the site of ancient and extensive chalk pits, is a gem of landscape gardening, and its tropical and subtropical collections are in high repute."* For Trevor this *"dearest and happiest spot"* remained his home until his death in 1897.

A flower mould.

The clean lines of the classic house set above the garden contrast with the Gothic Fountain, its flint and brick work hidden under water and ferns. The two are separated by Trevor's magnificent Medieval Wall.

Victorian pride delighted in a heraldic device – at the top of the Italian Terrace steps are two carved bricks with HMB. Records show that these were ordered in 1850 by Henry Bedingfeld whose wife's name was Mary, for the restoration of his walled kitchen garden at Oxburgh Hall. Perhaps Henry Trevor liked the idea of playing with his and his wife Eliza Mary's initials or maybe the stones were going cheap – the answer has yet to emerge.

A sweeping view back across the garden worthy of a Shakespearean performance.

Chapter Two

Recreation – The Victorian Artisan's Garden, Yalding

In 1993, HDRA – the Organic Organization commissioned me to design "A Green Chronology of Gardens" for their display gardens at Yalding in Kent. The visitor follows the development of the domestic garden from the medieval period to the opening of the twentieth century through six demonstration gardens. The fourth garden was to represent the nineteenth century, so I decided to design a *Victorian Artisan's Garden*, a neat urban or suburban garden which gave outward proof of its Victorian family's well-ordered lives as well as the potential of growing for show. The garden demonstrates the growing technology that followed the 1851 Great Exhibition matched by a greater availability of spare funds for luxuries such as greenhouses, cloches, and annual bedding plants to the keen nineteenth century householder.

The garden has three distinct areas: the *front garden* whose entrance is framed by neatly clipped yew trees, the paved path winds around a central seasonally planted circular bed; a *paved area* immediately behind (the non-existent house represented by treillage) with informal flowers and roses; the *vegetable garden* occupies the largest area with Victorian varieties of vegetables, fruit, and specialist flowers. A site has been allocated for a greenhouse. In 1998, an 1890s W. Richardson & Co., Darlington (Horticultural and Heating Engineers) greenhouse was donated which will be restored and erected. Even within this small area, the family has a choice of walks and areas in which to wander or sit. Let us join the imaginary tour.

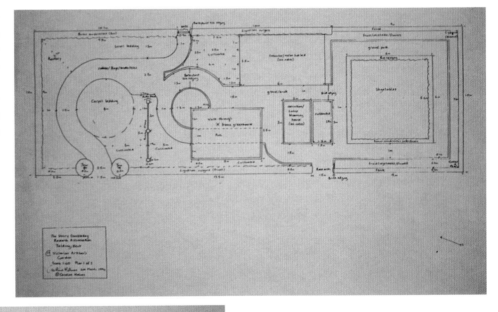

The ground plan for the Victorian Artisan's Garden; neat clipped hedges, showcase front garden, sitting area for the family leading to a prize winning vegetable patch.

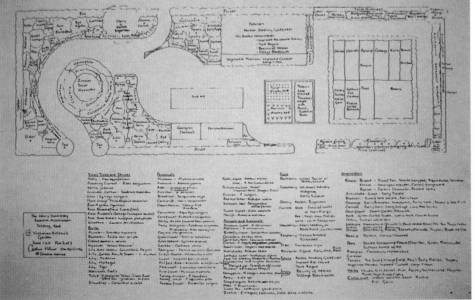

Planting plan for the Victorian Artisan's Garden; Victorian plant varieties and vegetables are provided by the HDRA Heritage Seed Library. Florist's flowers, whose perfect blooms could be entered into competitions include auriculas, *polyanthus*, pansies, carnations, picotees, pinks, *ranunculus*, and dahlias.

The Front Garden

Each year simplified carpet bedding has created colour and interest, my inspiration was from designs such as that illustrated in the Victorian Thompson's Gardeners Assistant. In 2001, the centenary of Victoria's death, I designed the carpet bedding around a VR and the dates of her accession 1837 and her death 1901. The silver background is provided by mass planting of *Cerastium tomentosum*, the letters are planted with *Begonia semperflorens* for V and *Salvia splendens* for R, the numbers with *Lobelia* "Crystal Palace," and the pompoms on the feet and tops of the letters with Heliotrope "Marine."

Victorian urban front paths often used attractive tiles with rope edge borders, an effect gained by the immaculate layout of these modern path bricks. The transition from formal front garden on show, to family back garden is marked by the rustic arbor.

A wet season can have a deleterious effect on the best planned bedding scheme!

2001 was the centenary of Victoria's death which was marked in the bedding scheme – the curvaceous style echoing the path's pattern.

The design was planted using stakes and string that subdivided the circle.

The plants were raised in pots, then thoroughly soaked. The planting hole was wetted and then planted. Dry soil was drawn up around the new plants so that no moisture would be lost through the soil surface by capillary action.

You can just about discern the "V" of dark leaves provided by *Begonia semperflorens* set on a silver background of *Cerastium tomentosum* and dates 1837 and 1901 in *Lobelia* "Crystal Palace."

The bedding in high summer. High rainfall created a cushioned rather than carpet effect. The regal purple pompoms on the V and R created out of flowering Heliotrope "Marine."

The Dwelling and its Immediate Surroundings

The division between the front and back gardens is represented by a crafted wooden arch and treillage with roses trained over them. The inspiration comes from one of the first fabrics produced by Morris, Marshal, Faulkner & Co. based on William Morris' own rose trellis at the Red House, Bexley Heath. Many Victorian varieties of roses and flowers are still available for the purist. A small area for leisure in an otherwise busy garden.

Several seed suppliers offer historic flower seed mixtures including the Victorian mix illustrated here.

1899 marked the bi-centenary of the introduction of the sweet pea into England. Victorian Henry Eckford bred a vast array of new varieties from 1870 as did the Burpee company in the United States.

The Vegetable and Fruit Garden

The original fruit and vegetable list was as follows. The plant names are all listed in Victorian references and, where possible, I have checked that they are still available. As far as the vegetables are concerned, they are provided from the HDRA Heritage Seed collection. Names are shown in alphabetical order both in contemporary common and Latin names.

Small trees

Cherry, Kentish Bigarreau
Elder, *Sambucus nigra*

Fruits

Blackberry, Wilson Junior or Parsley leaved
Cherry, Kentish Bigarreau
Currant, Black, Prince of Wales or Lee's Prolific
Currant, Red, Fay's New Prolific
Currant, White, White Transparent
Gooseberry, Whinham's Industry, Hedgehog, Early Sulphur
Raspberry, Yellow Antwerp
Raspberry, Fillbasket
Rhubarb, Elford, Early Red, Prince Albert
Strawberry, Keen's Seedling or Black Prince or Laxton's Noble

Vegetables

Artichoke, Globe, Early Purple
Beans, Broad, Dwarf Fan, Seville Longpod, Aquadulce, Windsor
Beans, French, Newington Wonder, Carter's Longsword
Beans, Runner, Carter's Champion, Painted Lady
Broccoli, Dwarf Late Purple, Early Cape
Cabbage, Early Brompton, Nonpareil, Early York, Savoy Little Prince
Cardoon
Carrots, Early Horn, Long Grange, Long Red Surrey
Cauliflower, Covent Garden Mammoth
Celery, Sutton's White Gem
Endive, Green Curled, Batavian
Garlic
Kale, Green, Curled Scotch, Welsh Kale, Chou de Russie
Lettuce, Hammersmith (for winter), Black seeded Brown Cos, Tom Thumb
Marrow, vegetable, Improved Custard, Large Cream
Onions, Strasbourg, Rocca, Naseby Mammoth, Tripoli, Blood Red, Globe
Parsnip, Students, Hollow Crowned
Peas, Double blossomed Frame/Charlton, Green Marrowfat, Suttons Latest of All
Potato, Kentish Seedling Goldfinder, Improved Ash Leaved Kidney, York Regent, Beauty of Hebron, Village Blacksmith
Radish
Rampion, Campanula rapunculus
Tomato, The Dwarf Orangefield, Key's Early Prolific, Trophy

Neat rows of Victorian vegetables and pinks in 1995, the first full year of production.

The thinking behind the fence in my design was that it could be used to support flowers and vegetables as well as fictional neighbors admiring the produce.

Outdoor tomatoes supported on a stout stick system as advocated by the 1881 *Thompsons Gardeners' Assistant*.

A Victorian artisan would probably not have paved around his vegetable plot; gravel and box edging were regarded as ideal. However, paving helps to create a micro-climate.

Herbs

Chives, *Allium schoenoprasum*
Dill, *Anethum graveolens*
Horseradish, *Cochlearia spp.*
Sweet Fennel, *Foeniculum vulgare*
Mint, *Mentha spicata*
Sweet Cicely, *Myrrhis odorata*
Basil, *Ocimum basilicum*
Marjoram, *Origanum onites*
Moss Curled Parsley, *Petroselenium crispum*
Rosemary, *Rosemarinus officinalis*
Green Sage, *Salvia officinalis*
Common Thyme, *Thymus vulgaris*

Victorian varieties of fruit and vegetables mostly ripen over a longer season which makes them more useful (and often better flavored) for the domestic household.

Horseradish was a popular Victorian condiment, the variegated leaf form is not as vigorous but just as delicious.

The bird scarer is made out of an old potato garnished with birds' feathers that is then attached to a flexible cane so that it appears to hover over the vegetables.

Chapter Three

Flower Gardens and Pleasure Grounds

Proprietors of small Victorian gardens read avidly about such pretensions and, although other writers advised against creating a floral toy shop, indulged in the pleasure of creating miniature versions with elaborate geometrical flower beds dotted about a modest lawn.

Just a year later in *An Irregular Villa in the Italian Style* Andrew Downing advocates: *Rustic seats placed here and there in the most inviting spots will both heighten the charm, and enable us to enjoy at leisure the quiet beauty around*.

The word parterres means "by the ground" and these low patterned box edged gardens enjoyed a great revival in the nineteenth century. *Holme Pierrepont Hall, Nottingham.*

Form and Ornament – Parterres

The term "parterre" literally translates as "by the ground," quite simply a flower bed but history has woven this term into living ornate scrolls and arabesques. The Victorian revival and, in France, restoration, of these seventeenth century masterpieces greatly influenced the layout of gardens around the house. Parterres were created on flat ground in elaborate geometric and flowing patterns mostly edged and hedged in Europe with dwarf box (*Buxus suffruticosa*) and in the States with *Ilex vomitaria*, filled with flowers or colored earth. They were viewed from the house and/or terrace. Some families would spell out their initials in the hedges or celebrate a national event. Designs for parterres fell into four main categories.

A close up of the beds in the parterre at Holme Pierrepont Hall. Note the box hedging has been cut to an edge so that snow cannot break the hedge. The hedging is infilled with lavender and spring bulbs such as tulips punctuating the billowing cushions of wallflowers.

> *To know all the different scenes which may be introduced in a pleasure-ground in modern times, it is only necessary to visit such a place as Alton Towers, in Staffordshire, where ... may be seen pagodas, hermitages, an imitation of Stonehenge, and of other Druidical monuments, shellwork, gilt domes, and huge blocks of mossy rock, bridges, viaducts, and many other curious objects.*
> —Mrs. Loudon, *The Ladies Companion to the Flower Garden*, 1841.

Parterre de compartiment – Compartmented parterres

The "compartiment" parterres were created as a unified design in reflecting boxed compartments, rather than an ensemble of separate patterns. Typically a square or rectangle is subdivided into four mirrored designs which are as effective when seen from above as alongside. The hedging outlining the more intricate designs was contrasted with low colorful flowers or stones, bricks, marble, sand, or clay.

The colorful compartmented parterre at Lyme Park could be sized down to good effect for a town garden.

Parterre de broderie – Embroidered parterres

The inspiration for the elaborate formations within the squares or rectangles from the "broderie" or embroidered parterres can be taken from needlework. Historically they were developed in marjoram, thyme, and lemon balm and then later elaborated with dwarf box hedging. Unlike the "compartment" parterres they are viewed on one axis only, preferably from the house and its terrace. They were ideal to scale down for front gardens or shady sides of a house.

The Victorian parterre at Holkham Hall designed by William Andrews Nesfield wrought in box (*Buxus sempervirens suffruticosa*) and grass has been woven into "flourishings" and "branchings" set off by white marble still look authentic in this early 1930's photograph. *Holkham Hall, Norfolk.*

The parterres at Holkham today, the hedges are neatly clipped but no white marble or topiary; height is provided by the urns.

Space permitting, the impact of the designs was emphasized by the "plat-bande," or border around the perimeter, of either sand edged with box hedging and a central flower bed (to show off new varieties) or grass with spaced topiary (yew, box, holly, and even spruce), statuary or tiles for ornate pots (citrus, bay, myrtle). Specialist lawn mowers were developed to cut the narrow bands of grass.

William Andrews Nesfield wrote for *The Gardeners' Chronicle* magazine describing how he designed his gardens. Many households created miniature versions of his ideas; this scrolling border can be scaled according to space and chosen plants.

Nesfield's scrolling beds have been simplified into box edged circles infilled with cotton lavender (*Santolina chamaecyparissus*). Note the cutwork detail in the grass under the plinth.

The patterns created in low box hedging could be in foliage shapes described as branchings, or flower shapes called flourishings. The center of the parterre featured intricate patterns and greatly influenced carpet bedding or mosaiculture.

Parterre à l'Anglaise – English patterned parterre

This "English" style parterre was an *entente cordiale* between the English love of turf and the French love of patterns. Historically, especially for those in dry climates, grasses were often mixed with chamomile, thymes, and other creeping plants for color and scent but unacceptable to Victorians seeking an immaculate green sward. The central turf bed could be a simple circle or square but some gardeners liked to create scallop, shell, and fan shapes, outlined and contrasted with white sand and box hedging. The designs could be minimized to act as a framework for topiary, statuary, or ornate pots.

The Grand Descent at Shrublands Hall was inspired by the Villa d'Este. Shrublands was noted for its head gardener Donald Beaton who created "harmonies" of color with finely selected floral shades.

The long terrace walk is punctuated with planting details that could be adapted for the smaller garden. A clematis swathed arbor stands between two conifers approached through two pairs of containers. The cordylines in the containers echo the coniferous spires. Similarly, the underplanting cascades like the clematis.

38

The former rosary is now called the Witches Circle (a stone edged basin) – one year planted soberly and another with garish exuberance.

Simple but effective. A circle of standard roses, underplanted with lavender around a plinth with planted urn.
(Also see illustration on page 11.)

Charles Barry also designed the parterres at Harewood House. Note the contrasting size and tone of the chipped stones and the ribbon of lawn that set off the shaped beds.

The box hedging acts like a coiling ribbon around the spring tulip and hyacinth bulbs.

The layout of the turf on the terrace at Osborne House looks like an arrangement of magic green carpets ready to lift off at any moment.

41

Parterres de pieces coupees pour les fleurs – Cut-work parterres

These parterres were glorified flower beds whose vibrant seasonal colors would brighten a dull summer's day, showing off the nurseryman and gardener's floral skills. Strictly no grass or colored earth was used, just flowers outlined with dwarf box hedging or clipped cushion forming plants like *Alternanthera* or *Sempervivums*. One Victorian gardening book suggests sowing acorns or holly berries thickly in a drill about two or three inches wide and keeping them trimmed to four or five inches high. He writes that this height could be maintained for some years – and I would add with considerable difficulty. In larger gardens, the area might be turfed and then dissected by paths or sanded strips for putting out pots, a design often adopted for rose gardens. This was ideal for the smallest Victorian garden or bedding schemes in municipal parks.

Queen Victoria (and indeed this continues today) would confer "Grace and Favour" apartments at Hampton Court Palace in recognition of royal services. In the 1880's one such resident, Ernest Law, introduced plantings that evoked the Tudor history of the Palace including this "knot" garden.

Claude Monet in his gardens at Giverny understood the trick of building up flowerbeds along a central spine to make a more dramatic floral effect.

42

A fall picture of the flower garden at Audley End that illustrates the patterned flower beds cut out of the smooth turf.

In summer, the bright annual and perennials in the flower garden at Audley End contrast with the "cloud" effect of the uncut yew backdrop.

The summer flowerbeds seem to dance around the central fountain at Audley End.

The dramatic colors and shapes of the geraniums, Ricinus, and Cannas are matched by the heady scent of Heliotrope, popularly known as Cherry Pie, in the Victorian garden of Calke Abbey.

The Victorian gardener would undoubtedly have disapproved of the daisies in the lawn but the circular bed of tulips and wallflowers is simple and effective.

Red Cannas add fire to the summer garden. Enhanced by a wire basket edging, this decorative feature also stops people stepping on your flowerbeds.

The perfect picture of a Victorian garden in high summer, this vista is framed by a *Trachycarpus* (Chusan Palm) on the left and basket edged pool on the right. The eye travels across the bedding to the plant theatre in the corner.

The term "gardensque" was coined by John Claudius Loudon early in the nineteenth century to describe decanting big ideas such as clumps of trees into domestic schemes with a specimen shrub or even pampas grass. Tatton Park decanted part of their grounds into a show garden for the 2000 Tatton Park Flower Show.

Austere but effective spring presentation of violas framed in geometric box hedging.

In 1899 C.E. Ponting designed this "skittles and balls" parterre of flowerbeds filled with Begonia *semperflorens* and *ageratum* surrounded by neat lawn, stonework, and topiary.

Chapter Four

Royal Residence – Osborne House, Isle of Wight

> *a place of one's own, quiet and retired…*
> —Queen Victoria, describing Osborne House,
> Isle of Wight

On her marriage to Prince Albert of Saxe-Coburg-Gotha, Queen Victoria had three royal residences: Windsor Castle with no private gardens, Buckingham Palace with nurseries in the attics, and the Royal Pavilion at Brighton which had neither nurseries nor gardens. So Victoria and Albert searched for a country retreat suitable for them and their growing family where they could escape court ceremonial. Osborne on the Isle of Wight set in three hundred forty two acres with a private beach for boating and bathing was ideal. In 1845 they bough the estate from Lady Isabella Blachford; further purchase finally brought the total to two thousand acres. The se ting reminded Albert of the Bay of Naples. He enthusia tically designed the house and grounds with the success ful builder Thomas Cubitt in Italianate style between 184 51. In 1846 Prince Albert planted a Magnolia grandiflo and the family stayed for the first time.

Queen Victoria's consort, Prince Albert, designed Osborne House with Thomas Cubitt in Italianate style – note the hallmark belvederes and pergola.

The upper and lower terraces were designed by Albert with Ludwig Gruner. The paving was made from a mid-nineteenth century composition called 'metallic lava,' a mix of tar, chalk, and gravel. The metallic lava was cleaned, polished, and then colored when laid: green for the upper terrace, blue by the main wing, and red and yellow on the lower terrace. The style is also Italianate but as an economic measure the balustrades and vases were molded in cement by Cubitt's workshops. The garden statuary was mostly factory-made cement or bronze-coated zinc casts of antique models, such as the boy with the goose. The Andromeda fountain on the upper terrace was by John Bell manufactured by the Coalbrookdale Foundry in 1851– the year of Albert's triumphant Great Exhibition. The triple arched alcove on the lower terrace often witnessed the Royal Family taking breakfast and where Victoria read and attended state papers, enjoying the scents of jasmine, orange blossoms, and roses from the nearby pergola.

The terrace parterre designed by Prince Albert and Ludwig Gruner with cement balustrades and vases molded by Cubitt's workshops were restored and replanted in 1997. The statue of the boy with the goose was a cast from a Roman original.

The tulips stand to attention in response to the strict order of the design.

A real sun trap where Queen Victoria took breakfast enjoying the summer scents of Jasmine, orange blossoms, and roses.

In 1850 the royal children were given vegetable plots, and on her birthday in 1854, Victoria gave them the furnished Swiss Cottage. The cottage was, in fact, constructed from the North American long-leafed pine, *Pinus strobus*, probably by the estate workers – there was a great fashion for imitation alpine chalets. In contrast to their royal upbringing, the children were encouraged to be market gardeners with their own set of gardening tools. Seeds were bought in and produce sold to the kitchen, all to be logged in their account books. The skeptic might add, "…and who tended the gardens when they were not living at Osborne?" The pragmatist might observe that they were learning the skills of delegation! They also created a museum to display their natural history and other collections. Adjoining the Swiss Cottage was an area known as the Victoria Fort and Albert Barracks, a miniature earth fort completed in 1856 with a drawbridge added in 1861.

The Swiss Cottage provided the royal family with a rustic cabin where their nine children each had vegetable and fruit patches.

Each child had their own monogrammed tools and wheelbarrow stored in this thatched shelter.

Twelve rectangular beds each, they sold the vegetables and fruit they raised to
the Royal kitchens. With the resulting income, they bought new seeds.

A rather upmarket scarecrow.

Chapter Five

Shaping Up – Flowerbeds

Victorian flowerbeds, just as today, ranged from deep borders to narrow strips but wherever possible pattern was introduced. The pattern can be in adapting the parterre patterns described in Chapter Three, within a circle, oval, square, or rectangle, or in shaping the outlines of the flowerbeds, but be warned against creating a mass of tadpoles and commas.

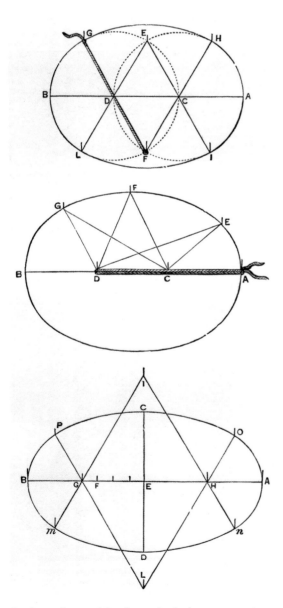

Ovals can be used for flower beds, lawns, or water features and harmonize well with any size or shaped garden.

A glance at our illustrations, which represent some of the best examples in the London parks in 1875, will show how cool strips of turf backed by verdant masses of trees and shrubs may be richly jewelled here and there with pleasing designs ... A number of geometrical forms are represented, such as are employed singly or in combination with others, and as suggestions it is assumed that they will be found useful to those who desire beds of particular pattern.
—Robert Thompson, *The Gardener's Assistant*, 1881.

When creating the flowerbeds, establishing the outline with edging bricks, tiles, stones or metal basket work will maintain the shape regardless of the inner planting. Framing metal basket or wicker work can be further enhanced with trained ivy, possibly even creating a handle frame for the ivy as well. Retaining shaped beds in grass is difficult unless properly redrawn every year. The oval is one of the simplest shapes and can be used for flowers, gravel, lawn, or water. According to Thompson, all you have to do is arm yourself with pegs and a line and follow his diagrams. I suggest doing this in miniature with a classroom compass, pencil, and cotton especially if your geometry is a bit rusty.

Accompanying an illustration very reminiscent of Nesfield designs (see page 37), Thompson wrote *In cases where it is desirable to have flower-beds on each side of a straight walk, curvilinear beds of the form represented are sometimes used, being less monotonous than a succession of straight-lined figures, even when these are connected together by circles. Formal subjects, as Cypresses, Irish Yews, trimmed Box, Portugal Laurel and Laurustinus, or standard roses, may be planted in the circles between the 'S' like beds.* For today, I propose that standard roses are ideal for the smaller garden as they can be bought in several heights and would look very attractive if the 'S' was underplanted with clove scented pinks (*Dianthus spp*) or lavender (*Lavandula spp*).

Sam Beeton improved and extended his *Shilling Gardener* into the alphabetical *Everyday Gardening*, describing plants from *Abies* to *Zostera* plus a monthly guide to tasks in the garden. Under "Beds" there is an excellent guide to creating the curvilinear shapes essential to the interesting Victorian garden. The detail may seem daunt-

Fuchsias can be used as seasonal or perennial bedding with their delicate foliage and hooped-skirt flowers.

ing to the modern reader used to information boxes and bullet points, but make a friend of the Victorian method which literally takes you step by step. Follow each instruction, one by one, (for "describe," the non-mathematician should read "draw") in the comfort of your armchair with compass, pencil, and paper. Then head confidently out to your cleared and raked ground armed with your trusty stakes, pegs, string, and rule.

Formation of Curvilinear Beds

Egg shaped or Ovate bed (indicated by solid line)

The method of forming an egg-shaped bed (shown in the diagram on page 55) will be found useful.

Set out the straight line AB equal to the greatest width of the bed required.

Divide it into two equal parts in the point C.

Through C draw the straight line DE, of indefinite length, at right angles to AB.

From point C, where AB and DE intersect with each other with the radius CA or CB, describe the circle AFB.

Taking A and B as centers, with AB and BA as radii, describe the arcs BH, AK, and from the same points A and B, draw through G - one of the points in which the circle AFBG cuts the straight line DE.

Straight lines AL, BM cutting the arc BH in the point O, and the arc AK in the point N.

Lastly from G as center, with the radius GN or GO, describe the arc or quarter circle NO.

The bedding fuchsias in the fall at Wimpole Hall, their red flowers set off by the bright green turf and dark yew outer hedging.

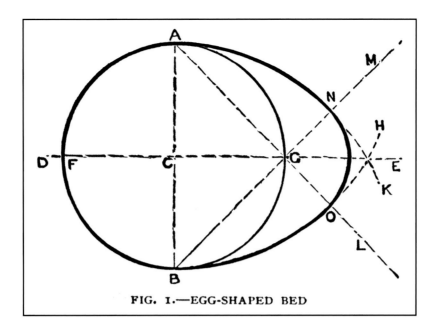

FIG. I.—EGG-SHAPED BED

Magnificent fuchsias. Victorian flower shows were held several times a year as a showcase to inspire and encourage the home gardener to greater achievements.

Bed of semicircles on sides of square

Lay out two straight lines, AB and CD intersecting each other at right angles in E.

From E as center, with any length of radius that may be determined upon, describe the circle FGHK.

In this circle inscribe a square, also FGHK.

From points L, M, N, O, where sides of square intersect with straight lines AB, CD, describe the arcs FPG, GQH, HRK, KSF.

A bed of the form shown by the solid arcs of circles will then be formed, consisting of four semicircles described on the four sides of a square.

Note: The simplest method of construction is to lay out a square first of all, as FGHC, next to bisect the four sides of the square in the points L, M, N, O, and from these points as centers to describe the semicircles FPG, GQH, HRK and KSF, that form the bed; but the more elaborate mode of procedure has been given because it is suggestive of the formation of other beds - as a crescent, formed by the solid arc FPG and the dotted arc FG, which is a fourth part of the circumference of the circle FGHK. Other forms are those which are bounded by the solid arc FPG, and the dotted arcs FE, GE, or by the dotted arcs FG, GE, EF.

Semicircular ribbon or horseshoe bed

Draw a straight line, AB, equal in length to the distance between the outer edges of the border and this is divided into any number of equal parts, according to the width of the bed that it is intended to make.

In this case it is divided into four equal parts, in the points C, D, and E.

From the center, D, at the distance, DA, describe the semicircle AHB, and from the same center at the distance DC describe the semicircle CKE.

Bisect the lines AC, EB, in the points F and G, and from these points as centers, with the radii FA and GB, describe the semicircles ALC, BME, which complete the end of the bed

Note: A bed of horseshoe form may be produced by extending the circumferences of the circles AHB, CKE, and forming the extremities of the bed, by drawing straight lines as DN, DO, intersecting the circumference of the circles. From Fig. 3, it may be easily seen how to form a bed of an **S**, or serpentine form, by repeating the process already described on the line AB produced towards A or B, or continuing it on the lines DN or DO produced towards N or O.

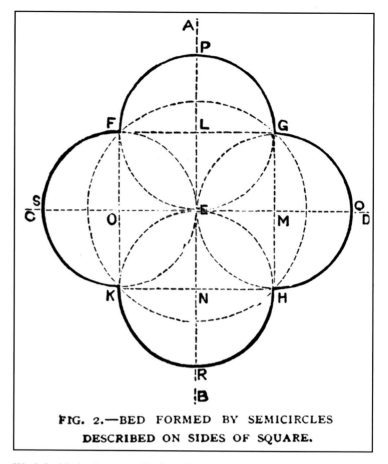

FIG. 2.—BED FORMED BY SEMICIRCLES DESCRIBED ON SIDES OF SQUARE.

Work inside in the warm firstly with paper, rule, and compass, then prepare the clean earth canvas and arm yourself with measure, stakes, and string. Precise attention to measurements at this stage will ensure exquisitely sinuous flowerbeds.

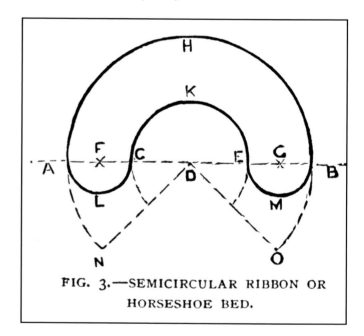

FIG. 3.—SEMICIRCULAR RIBBON OR HORSESHOE BED.

Curves in the garden landscape! The gravel path meanders by the oval flower bed, domed tree, and over the small iron bridge in the winter landscape at the Swiss Garden.

The delightful layout of circular and crescent beds at Lyme Park could be effectively scaled down for seasonal or perennial planting. The standard roses at each corner provide delicate height and symmetry.

Keeping the definitions between planting patterns can prove difficult; if you look carefully you will see that each plant row is separated by a metal edging.

If you are unsure about which patterns to choose, experiment with annuals. If you do not like the finished product, dig it in at the end of the season and start afresh.

Serpentine bed

Mark out a straight line AB, equal to the length of the bed from end to end.

Divide into 3 equal parts in the points C and D.

Divisions AC, DB are again subdivided into two equal parts in the points E and F.

From E and F as centers with radii EA, FB, the semi-circles AGC, BHD, are described.

From C and D as centers, with radii CA and DB, the semi-circles AKD, BLC, are described, completing the outline of the bed.

By dividing AB into two equal parts in M, and from M as center, with the distance MA on MB, describing the dotted circle ANBO, a bed of a curved pear shaped form is obtained, as AGCLBO.

Another form of serpentine bed

Straight line AB is divided into three equal parts, and each of these parts is again subdivided in E, G, and F.

Perpendiculars on opposite sides of AB are erected to AB at E and F, as EH and FK.

In EH, take EL, equal to EA or EC, and in FK take FM, equal to FB or FD.

Join LM, and from L through C draw LN, and from M through D draw MO.

Then from L as center, with radius LC, describe the arc ACP, and from M as center, with radius MD, describe the arc BDQ, and next from the same centers, with radii LQ, MP, describe the arcs QR, PS.

Join AR, BS, and bisect them in T and U.

Create perpendiculars TV, UX, to AR, BAS, at the points T and U, and from V and X (where these perpendiculars cut LR, MS) as centers with radii VR, XS, describe the arcs AR, BS, which complete the figure.

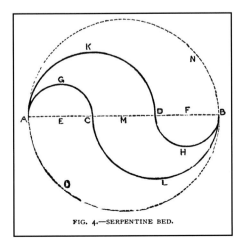

FIG. 4.—SERPENTINE BED.

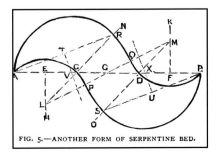

FIG. 5.—ANOTHER FORM OF SERPENTINE BED.

Cordate or heart-shaped bed

Divide line AB into four equal parts in the points D, C, E.

Taking D and E as centers, with radii DA and DB, the semicircles AFC, CGB, are described.

From same points as centers describe the arcs BLH, AKH with radii BD, EA which intersect each other in H.

Note: By dividing AB into six equal parts in the points M, N, C, O, P, and by describing the semicircle AQB from C as center, with radius CA or CB, and the semi-circles ATN, NRO, and OVB, from M, C, and P as centers, a fan-shaped figure enclosed by dotted lines is obtained, and by completing the circle AQBS, a bed similar to that shown by the diagram for the horseshoe bed.

Note: By the larger and small semicircles disposed about the straight line AB, a bird like figure, with symmetrical wings, is shown; and another bed, bounded by the semicircles AFC, CGB, above the line AB and the semicircle ASB below it.

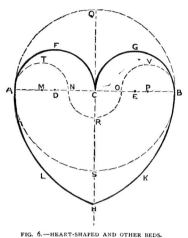

FIG. 6.—HEART-SHAPED AND OTHER BEDS.

Hearts and flowers or perhaps hearts and grass or just a garden of love.

Cordate herbs and topiary. The heart is filled with sage, the hedges are dwarf box, the topiary, yew, and the outer fillings gravel and santolina.

Shakespeare's words inspired Victorian paintings and gardens. Take some lines from Henry V:

A speaker is but a prater, a rhyme is but a ballad; a good leg will fall, a straight back will stoop, a black beard will turn white, a curl'd pate will grow bald, a fair face will wither, a full eye will wax hollow: but a good heart, Kate, is the sun and the moon, or rather the sun and not the moon; for it shines bright, and never changes, but keeps his course truly.

The heart shaped beds in the illustrations at Squerryes Court and Villandry are good and bright. You could also introduce moonlit brightness by planting up with white flowers. Savor Andrew Downing's suggestion for a summer moonlight walk: *"the silence broken only by the gentle murmur of the fountain…and see, softly gleaming in the silvery beams, the sculptured vases clustered over partially by luxuriant climbers, and backed by dark masses of rich waving shrubs and flowers…"*

Joachim Carvallo and his American wife, Ann, recreated Renaissance gardens at Villandry in 1906. This parterre symbolizes "Tender Love" – pink hearts, lips whispering sweet nothings, and red flames of passion.

A simple posy of spring flowers at Longue Vue in New Orleans.

The language of flowers, much used by Shakespeare, enjoyed a great Victorian revival, for example roses, the flowers of love, poetry and beauty, have no less than thirty-four meanings. A red rose means *I love you* but a deep red rose *bashful shame*; a rosebud *young and innocent love* and a white rose *silence, I am worthy of you;* whilst the wilder eglantine (or sweetbrier) is a symbol of true love because it survives happiness and adversity.

Instead of box hedging in warmer zones you could use myrtle (*Myrtus communis*), the plant of love and beauty, sacred to Venus, sprigs of which were carried by Queen Victoria in her wedding bouquet. Cuttings were taken of the myrtle in this bouquet and the bushes still survive at Osborne. Other edgings might be Rosemary for remembrance and fidelity in love, or Ivy (*Hedera*) for friendship, fidelity, and marriage, or Periwinkle (*Vinca*) for happy recollections.

A sweetly scented Victorian summer mixture – lavender and heliotrope.

How about the sweetly scented pinks and carnations? Deep red flowers represent *alas for my poor heart*, whilst striped are *refusal* and yellow *disdain*. Spring ushers in straightforward sentiments with the tulip representing the lover's blushing countenance and hot coals of desire; the blue hyacinth a symbol of fidelity, and pansies for thoughts and heartsease. A final Shakespearean green sentiment from *A Winter's Tale*: *"For you there's rosemary and rue; these keep seeming and savour all the winter long; Grace and remembrance be to you both."*

A final assortment of shapes for flowerbeds, grass, or water. Remember less is more – one decent sized bed is more effective than a myriad pocket handkerchief beds.

Carpet Bedding

As the name suggests, plants are woven into a ground hugging pattern; this form of gardening is mostly now confined to public parks and gardens. It was said "rich people used to show their wealth by the size of their bedding plant list; 10,000 for a squire, 20,000 for a baronet, 30,000 for an earl and 50,000 for a duke." In 1890 the Rothschilds used 51,000, at Waddesdon in 2002 they used 230,000 for the recreated schemes. These compact designs are labor-intensive but ideal for small urban front gardens that want to create an authentic nineteenth century look. They are best planted as plugs so that they grow into a cohesive design.

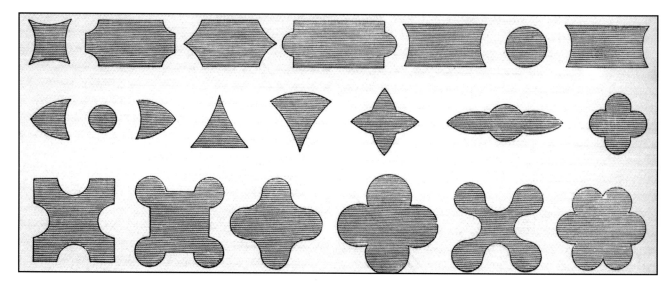

Carpet bedding. A circular centerpiece or rectangular rug – see the black and white illustration on page 64. Note the intricate detail created with just the texture of plants.

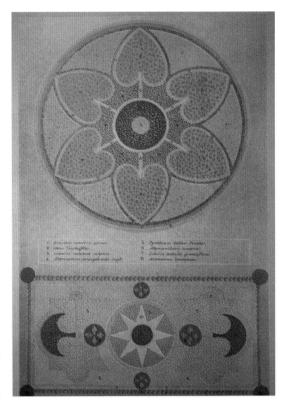

Five arrows representing the five founding brothers of the European Rothschild dynasty.

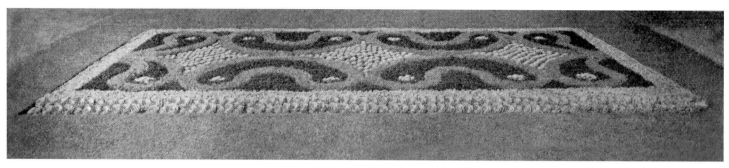

Succulents such as Echeveria and *Sempervivum* are ideal for such elaborate designs.

Above and opposite page:
The ornate Victorian parterre at Waddesdon inspired this demonstration bed of
suitable plants, e.g. varieties of *Alternanthera*.

"TRIAL BED"

The range of plants within this area are
being appraised for use within the
seasonal displays in future years

The effect is like a scatter cushion edged in dwarf *Helichrysum* and filled with *ageratum* and *impatiens*.

Rich fun! The aviary and the bird would be prohibitively expensive but the basket ironwork and raised bed within are possibilities and would provide an excellent stage for a Victorian statue or container.

Tropical Splendor

Tropical plants were imported via Botanical Gardens around the world to be used in magnificent tropical displays. In gentler zones the hardier bananas, cannas, and palms will overwinter outside or with light protection.

The effect should be dramatic from enormous leaves and bright underplanting. If you have frost proof protection either under glass or a well lit outhouse, the perennial plants can remain in large pots. Literally, after the last frost, sink the pots into the prepared earth and cover, reversing the process at the end of the season.

Tropical splendor. Exciting foliage effects from *Musa*, *Trachycarpus,* and *Canna* offset by bright bedding all framed by ironwork.

Small bed, great effect – *Musa*, *Canna*, and *Chlorophytum*.

Garden Theatre

During the eighteenth century, auricula theatres were built into corners of walled gardens; they remained popular through the nineteenth century and are currently enjoying a revival. The theatre can be used to protect blooms from being damaged by the sun and the display should be changed seasonally. The theatre illustrated is at Calke Abbey and is on a suitably large scale. This can be repli-cated to the size of a puppet theatre or reinterpreted as staging in a conservatory, up the steps leading to the house, or around a small pool. The pots need to be terracotta, as the temperature and conditions in plastic or ceramic pots tends to fluctuate which greatly disadvantages the plants. How to keep the pots watered should be one of your first thoughts. One solution is standing each in a small terracotta dish which will not be detrimental to their appearance and eases the task.

A grand theatre originally constructed to house auriculas but also perfect for geraniums and which can be scaled down for smaller corners.

Geraniums were popular Victorian flowers in the ground, trained up conservatory walls, or in pots.

A delightful free standing Victorian conservatory inviting the gardener to while away hours tending the flowers.

The central tiered show piece attracts the eye away from the working areas in the conservatory.

My husband built the wall in our garden with two south-east facing niches for plant displays opposite the kitchen window. Small but delightful, they enjoy morning sun until about midday; on Christmas or celebratory winter evenings we use them for night lights. He always searches out old materials and in this case the bricks are actually eighteenth century, but I am still waiting for him to put the capping on the wall!

Brickwork makes an attractive setting for Victorian town gardens such as the one shown on page 72 in Bury St. Edmunds. Our local town of Bury St. Edmunds has an open garden scheme in June which provides wonderful practical inspiration just as across the ocean in New Orleans they regularly have gardens open days in the French Quarter - another stunning source of ideas. Garden opening schemes are run as fund raisers throughout the United Kingdom and the United States, styles and tastes are eclectic with most owners only too happy to share their tips if not their secrets.

We have two niches opposite our kitchen window that provide two mini theatres – the winter setting with snow topping the box topiaries.

The larger stage of a private garden in Bury St. Edmunds, Suffolk.
Four box topiaries take the lead around the central sundial.

A small theatrical company – a topiary box with two auriculas.

Before looking at Biddulph Grange I will leave you with an extract from Mrs. Loftie's 1879 *Social Twitters*:

It is often amusing to trace a fashion as it percolates downwards. By the time it has reached the far-away sleepy country villages something quite new and entirely opposite is really the rage amongst the upper ten thousand. Cottagers now try to fill their little plots with geraniums and calceolarias, which they are obliged to keep indoors at great inconvenience to themselves and loss of light to their rooms. Meantime my lady at the Court is hunting the nursery grounds for London Pride and gentianella to make edgings in her wilderness, and for the fair tall rockets, the cabbage roses, and nodding columbines which her pensioners have discarded and thrown away.

Chapter Six

A World of Gardens – Biddulph Grange, Staffordshire

> *By a happy arrangement of the surface of the ground and its formation into an infinite variety of hills and dales, nooks and recesses, a considerable amount of shelter and exposure, sunniness and shade, dryness and moisture, has been obtained in the most ingenious manner; and the plants selected and the positions adopted for them with a patient study of their wants and a careful regard for their healthy development, which takes the visitor completely by surprise.*
>
> —Edward Kemp, *Gardeners' Chronicle* 1856

Biddulph Grange belonged to the Bateman family who had bought this estate and neighboring Knypersley in Staffordshire for their mineral and industrial potential. The Bateman family fortune was funded by coal mines, ironworks, and cotton mills. In 1837, Bateman, when still only 26, had published the first part of his *Orchidaceae of Mexico and Guatemala*, the largest botanical book ever produced; five further parts were published over the next six years.

Biddulph Grange is a large, ugly house – any property large or small, ugly or pretty, is enhanced when mirrored in water.

A winter vista across the "Italian" Garden – the hedges, gravel, and turf providing an austere pattern.

By 1840, when James Bateman, his wife, Maria and their two sons moved into Biddulph Grange, gardens and especially orchids exercised a far greater interest. James was, as noted, an orchid collector and expert. He and Maria shared a passion for ferns and Maria predates Gertrude Jekyll in her knowledgeable arrangement of herbaceous borders. James Bateman was a Fellow of the Royal Society and he and Maria enjoyed a wide circle of horticultural and botanical friends, exchanging plants and ideas, and funding plant and orchid hunting expeditions.

Bateman was inspired by Prince Albert and Thomas Cubbitt's work at Osborne when extending Biddulph Grange. The Italianate house sported not just an adjoining conservatory but a Roman inspired peristyle or court garden, a rhododendron house that later became the fern house, orangery, and a camellia house. The large, ugly house we see today is the restored remnants following a fire in 1896. Another influence that today's collector can still use, was the nearby Minton Hollins tile factory in Stoke on Trent. Herbert Minton was an orchid enthusiast and his tiles were used in the house and garden.

In 1847 Bateman met the marine artist and keen gardener Edward Cooke, also a fern enthusiast, collecting them from the wild and designing fern houses and cases. At Biddulph, Cooke probably designed all the architectural features in the garden as well as the rockwork for the fernery and used the upturned roots of dead trees to form a "stumpery". The Italianate inspired designs of the house were carried into the terraced gardens framing the house that took the visitor out to view the lake or up to the distant Wellingtonia Avenue. Beyond the lake lies the world of plants that were newly available via nurseries such as Loddiges in Hackney, London, which were sought by knowledgeable, talented owners such as the Batemans.

Wealthy Victorians collected the array of newly introduced rhododendrons whose blooms painted hillsides into a sea of color. Beyond the Himalayas, plants were also arriving from the Far East and Australia. Chinese designs and styles had already been popularized in eighteenth century gardens. At Biddulph, Cooke designed a "Great Wall of China" to disguise and protect the gardens that look like a Chinese Willow pattern service. The romantic appeal of "Cathay," the old name for China, had been popularized by the Staffordshire blue and white transfer Willow pattern wares of Josiah Spode and Joshua Heath.

The lower terrace overlooks the "Italian" lake with Himalayan rhododendrons beyond. Wealthy Victorians avidly collected the array of newly introduced rhododendrons – not forgetting the Monkey Puzzle trees on the terrace.

A glimpse over the "Great Wall of China" which disguises and protects the Chinese inspired gardens sporting temples, bridges, terraces, and plantings

Through the vast stone doorway looms a gilded ox with a solar disc between its horns gazing over the Chinese Waters. Pagoda roofs have sharp ends to catch any dragons that tried to slide down – how about a tame dragon in the lawn instead?

As you enter the vast stone doorway you look up to a gilded ox with a solar disc between its horns which in turn gazes over the Chinese Waters, looking like the bronze ox in the Summer Palace outside Beijing. The bright colors and ornate fretwork of the buildings and bridges provide the Chinese backdrop for the newly introduced azaleas (now rhododendrons), Moutan peonies, roses, and chrysanthemums (now Dendranthemum). The gardeners had endless problems getting the Moutan peonies to thrive.

Bush peonies had been popular garden plants since medieval times but these new "tree" peonies were highly prized. There is a surviving golden larch (*Pseudolarix amabilis*) which was actually introduced by Robert Fortune from China. Cooke designed the waters to leave China via a Scottish glen; a walk through the rockwork took the visitor past the Cheshire Cottage incongruously surrounded by Chinese junipers (also introduced by Robert Fortune), to another ancient land – Egypt.

The Temple and Terrace. Chinese fashioned garden buildings bring color, interest, and intrigue into the gardens.

View from the Temple to the bridge and in the far right upper corner the Joss House, an English collector's garden speaking with a Chinese accent.

Dragon or any other beast will need to be outlined in metal,
preferably below the cutting blades of your lawn mower.

A tall beech hedge and a screen of yews kept the Egyptian court disguised until the last moment; as you turned between golden and common yew clipped to represent stone obelisques and a pair of stone sphinxes. Inside the "pyramid" is a statue of the Ape of Thoth, an associate of the god Thoth who the Egyptians credited with inventing botany.

The golden and common yew are clipped to represent stone obelisks as you enter the temple past the stone sphinx.

A living cloche! Cotoneaster has been clipped and trained around the base of an allee of Crab apple trees.

A "containerized" tree that has long outgrown its ornate pot and become a permanent feature.

Charles Darwin was a friend of James and Maria Bateman. He lived at Down House in Kent from 1842 to 1882 where he combined family and intellectual life. His work on evolution was refuted by Bateman and inspired Edward Cooke to publish *Grotesque Animals* in 1872 adding "...*These oddities, from fancy drawn, May surely raise the question, will DARWIN say - by Chance they're formed, Or Natural Selection.*"

At Down House, Darwin created his "thinking-path" around the gardens and built several greenhouses to study his collections of orchids, many supplied by Bateman, and carnivorous plants. He predicted the pollinator for the Comet Orchid (*Angraecum sesquipidale*) forty years before it was proved, based on his theory of evolution through natural selection.

Charles Darwin was a great friend of James and Maria Bateman. He lived at Down House from 1842 to 1882 where he combined family and intellectual life.

He created his "thinking-path" around the gardens and built several greenhouses for the collections of orchids and carnivorous plants that he studied.

He predicted the pollinator for the Comet Orchid (*Angraecum sesquipidale*) forty years before it was proven, based on his theory of evolution through natural selection.

Orchids in Michael Bowell's conservatory in Pennsylvania.

Biddulph was a show case for the plants and styles that impressed the Batemans, a principle that can be adopted in the smallest garden. Good gardening practice is to check the origins of any plant you plan to grow. How imaginative to take that a stage further and recreate a pocket of China, Egypt, or India. The upturned tree root provides a sculpted base for spring and shade loving ferns and other plants. Clipped topiary can create a veritable army, menagerie, or aviary set in different gravels or on patterned paving. Bringing plants in and around the house under glass, in interesting containers, and hanging baskets creates a verdant transition between house and garden.

Traditional orchid box for epiphytic orchids at the University Botanic Gardens, Cambridge.

Five Victorian orchid pots – a nest of pots from seed to tree and two forcers – sea kale and rhubarb. In the States, ornamental terracotta vases were produced at the Salamander Works, Cannon Street, New York or in artificial stone at Gibson's or Goodwin's Warehouses.

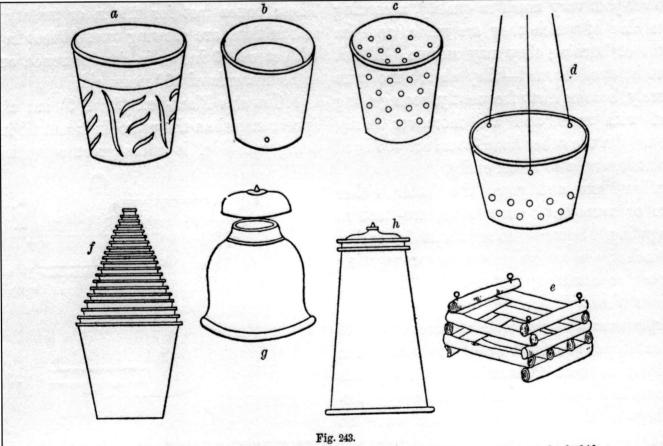

Fig. 243.

a, Orchid pot. b, Orchid pot (loose bottom). c, Perforated Orchid pot. d, Shallow suspending pan for Orchids. e, Suspending Orchid basket. f, Nest of pots, 1¾ to 30 inches. g, Sea-kale pot. h, Rhubarb pot.

Pleasing clean line formality in this arrangement of pots, clipped box in gravel on a small brick raised platform.

Using terracotta pots avoids extremes of heat and cold, damp and drought; however, they are lost in the exuberance of their planting in this tiered display

Many Victorian garden encyclopedias encourage gardeners to plant up hanging baskets with spring bulbs, hyacinths, and narcissus, just like this one recently created for the Philadelphia Flower Show.

Victorian magazines and encyclopedias encouraged do-it-yourself and these two containers show great individual taste – the first for bright summer annuals and the second for alpines.

Chapter Seven

The Victorian Art and Craft of Garden Making

William Morris, Augustus Pugin, and John Ruskin believed in *the Gothic principles of evolving our homes out of local conditions and requirements* so if you live in an area with naturally occurring rocks, pave with local flags, alternatively use bricks, flints, or pebbles. Stories and plantlore from the Bible, the Medieval period, and Shakespeare inspired romance and chivalry in garden design, patterns, textures, and planting. Gardens sported rustic work arbors, bowers, and arches with trailing scented vines, reminiscent of Shakespeare's *A Midsummer Night Dream:* "...*with luscious woodbine, with sweet musk-rose and with eglantine...*"

Very much a home made set of steps using local wood crafted into fence, rails, and treads.

William Robinson believed a garden should grow out of its own site and he used timber and stone from local supplies to make rustic work bridges and furniture, stone seats, and brick trellises. He advocated using native and hardy American plants in the pages of his many books, *The Garden* magazine, and through his craftsman-like approach. In the United States, gardeners were advised to plant hedgerows of thorns such as the Newcastle thorn, *a native sort, much hardier and better than the English for our climate.* Artists such as the keen Cotswold gardener Alfred Parsons, and Mark Fisher, H.A. Olivier, and H.G. Moon all painted at Gravetye Manor where Robinson also entertained Edward Burne-Jones and John Ruskin.

Gertrude Jekyll met William Robinson in 1875 and appreciated this "natural" gardening. In 1883 she bought fifteen acres of Munstead Heath, opposite her mother's house, just outside Godalming in Surrey, to create her own garden. Incidentally, also in 1883, the Impressionist artist Claude Monet moved into the village of Giverny in Normandy and started to create his inspirational gardens. In 1889 she met and started to foster the talents of the young Edwin Lutyens, whose vernacular but stark designs were enhanced and softened by their accompanying Jekyll gardens. Lutyens initially designed her a small house cum workshop which she called "The Hut." In 1897, after the death of her mother, Lutyens designed Munstead Wood House whose sympathetic use of the local hard sandstone, Bargate stone, created a building that seems to grow out of its own site. Every window and door is individually crafted and the overhanging jetty that looks down onto a courtyard and the garden beyond provides a timeless quality. A delightful detail is the swags of clematis trained along the under edge of the jetty.

Munstead Wood house in the fall illustrates the sympathetic use of local materials to create a building that grows out of its own site.

95

Rosemary and Senecio billowing against the south facing house front.

Swags and steps – Jekyll disliked slopes in a garden always advocating steps in local materials softened by planting. The jetty is delightfully decorated with a swag of clematis.

Sitting on the Lutyens seat, the view is narrowed by clipped hedges before being released into the verdancy beyond.

On the south front, mass plantings of Rosemary and Senecio billow, attractively lining the path to the driveway and front door. The paths and terraces use a mixture of materials, the narrow end of tiles used in paving makes an excellent non-slip surface as well as providing pleasing detail. Jekyll disliked slopes in a garden always advocating steps in local materials softened by plantings. The view from the courtyard under the jetty is narrowed by clipped hedges before being released into the verdancy beyond.

The Jekyllian hallmarks – pergola and a long border of drifting herbaceous plants and shrubs.

Inspired by the artist J.W.M. Turner, Jekyll perfected a painterly use of herbaceous plants and shrubs in summer borders to demonstrate her ideas of drifting color. In the Long Border at Munstead Wood, designed to be at its best in June and July, the colors drift from silvery blues to a crescendo of reds and yellows in the center and then cooling off as the border reaches the pergola. Jekyll chose her colors carefully and often included tamarisk whose *"pink haze… acts as a lacy screen."* She gave the following advice to gardeners seeking impressionistic effects in their borders:

Orange – the effect is bright and hot, sufficient to visually warm up any grey day, so the oranges veer towards red not yellow.

Grey – the effect is grey-green and silver grey with flowers of white, pastel pink and blues.

Gold – gold plants veer towards lighter yellows not oranges.

Blue – blues veer towards white and grey, not purple, but the pink haze of the tamarisk acts as a screen.

Green – shades, shape and texture of foliage with white flowers.

The colors drift from silvery blues to a crescendo of reds and yellows in the center and then cooling off as the border reaches the pergola.

A Jekyll maintenance tip – maintain a narrow path along the back of a deep border so that you can tie up, replant, and prune from behind thereby causing minimal visible damage.

Her Long Border at Munstead Wood is backed by a Bargate stone wall providing protection and height. She softened the wall with small trees and tall shrubs separated from the main herbaceous border by a narrow path. This gave Jekyll and her gardeners easy access for maintenance and prevented the trees and shrubs leeching too much goodness from the borders.

Between 1894 and 1912 Jekyll and Lutyens undertook some seventy gardens in partnership. Lutyens designed and built houses using local materials in textural harmony with their surrounding countryside that in turn were echoed in the architectural layout and detailing of their gardens. Jekyll filled this framework with artistic plantsmanship, perfecting color schemes in long herbaceous borders and softening walls and terraces with climbing and scrambling plants. Jekyll advised her clients to plant for seasonal rather than year round effect, so within the garden she would design separate spring, June, August, autumn, and winter gardens, each to be savored at their zenith. In a small garden, this can be achieved by clever manipulation of flowerbeds using bulbs and evergreens to carry the overall display through the year.

In 1908, Charles Holme, founder of *The Studio* magazine approached Jekyll to design gardens around his newly restored The Manor, Upton Grey. The terraced gardens lying to the south of the Manor and the Wild Garden to the north are textbook examples of her work, beautifully restored by the present owners John and Rosamund Wallinger. The short pergola, swathed in the roses Blush Rambler and Seagull, Jasmine, and Aristolochia, demonstrate how effective even a small pergola can be. The pergola is made out of stout wooden posts with swags of thick rope between – a hefty rope only to be found in a chandlers yard. Equally, the borders are foreshortened by the terracing but still manage to achieve Jekyll's hallmark floral crescendo.

The short pergola at The Manor, Upton Grey, is swathed in the roses Blush Rambler and Seagull, Jasmine and Aristolochia. The plants are trained up the wooden posts and along swags of thick rope.

The Italianate style use of clipped box is too stiff for most Arts and Crafts styles so Jekyll favored *Bergenia*, popularly known as Elephant's Ears, as an edging. The stone seat at The Manor, Upton Grey backed with *Viburnum tinus*, demonstrates this simple usage admirably and more importantly invites the gardener to rest and enjoy the fruits of his labor.

Rosamund Wallinger has achieved Jekyll's floral crescendo in the shorter east facing border at The Manor, Upton Grey.

Herbaceous borders can be simplified to billowing clumps of delphiniums, campanulas and alchemilla.

Opposite page:
Jekyll advised keeping a back up stock of
annuals and sweet peas to train into the gaps
left by early flowering plants.

Bergenia, popularly known as Elephant's Ears, are one of Jekyll's favorite edging plants. This seat backed with
Viburnum tinus invites the gardener to rest and enjoy the fruits of his labor.

There is a small paved courtyard in front of The Manor, Upton Grey which leads to the Wild Garden. Here the steps are formed from grass and are broadly curvaceous, gently preparing you for the mown grass paths, walnut, and other nut trees and unusual bamboo grove. Charles Holme was fascinated by Japanese design and the shape and practicality of bamboo captured the imagination of many Arts and Crafts followers.

Sweeping grass steps mark the transition from the hard landscaping of the house courtyard to the Wild Garden designed by Jekyll.

A favorite Victorian sentiment that can be found on The wall that divides the Spring from Summer gardens at Munstead Wood.

Jekyll was an early exponent of photography, leaving detailed records of her own gardens, early nineteenth century life in West Surrey villages, and her tours. An interesting example was the walled remains of Edzell Castle's garden which had been created for Sir David Lindsay and Dame Isobel Forbes in 1604. The surrounding walls were as much a part of the garden as the central planting. Jekyll noted and admired the regular checkerboard design in the walls which would be ideal for planting. Garden history excels when used to cherry pick designs that work just as well centuries later. The dry stone and other walls created by Arts and Crafts garden makers were left with cracks and crevices to host plants for each and every aspect from shady ferns to sunny thymes.

Jekyll photographed Edzell Castle's walled garden before it was restored and commented about the excellent potential it had for planting.

Arts and Crafts garden makers left cracks and crevices in the walls to host plants for each and every aspect, as can be seen here at The Manor, Upton Grey.

The later Italianate style of Reginald Blomfield and Harold Peto, at the end of the nineteenth century, was also applauded by Jekyll. Blomfield was the first to use the term "formal" for gardens. He and Peto used plants to soften the terraces and balustrades of earlier Victorian Italianate gardens. Jekyll remained on good terms with both Robinson and Blomfield using the best of formal styles with vernacular materials.

Throughout the Victorian period, books were published to guide and encourage men and women to improve their homes and gardens. In 1842 Andrew Downing described his householders:

> *The master of the premises we shall suppose capable of managing the kitchen garden, the fruit trees, the grass, and the whole of the walks, himself, with perhaps the assistance of a common gardener, or labouring man, for a day or two, at certain seasons of the year. The mistress and her daughter, or daughters, we shall suppose to have sufficient fondness for flowers, to be willing and glad to spend three times a week, an hour or two, in the cool mornings and evenings of summer, in the pleasing task of planting, tying to neat stakes, picking off decayed flowers, and removing weeds from the borders, and all other operations that so limited a garden may require.*

Mr. Shirley Hibberd published *Rustic Adornments for Homes of Taste* in 1856 as a guide to home (and self) improvements for the middle classes *without the help of a garden, it is impossible to cultivate chaste ideas and refining feelings*. Jekyll carved wood, inlaid with mother of pearl, produced gorgeous embroidery, and was consummately talented. However, for the less practical followers of the Arts and Crafts philosophy almost every village had a carpenter or bodger who could fashion "rustic" features for the garden from the local woods or a blacksmith to forge ironwork.

Wealthy Victorian magnates like Lord Armstrong at Cragside created vast rockeries out of the local outcrops.

Even the smallest garden could create planted fissures.

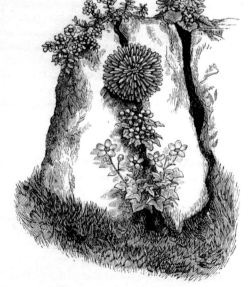

Fig. 417.—Method of planting Fissures.

Henry Trevor trained ivy over his Medieval Wall in a pattern similar to that used at The Dairy, Waddesdon Manor. Canes are used to maintain and train the ivies into this diamond pattern.

TROPÆOLUM LOBBIANUM.

Balustrades created the desired Italianate effect in early Victorian gardens softened as the twentieth century approached with swathes of planting.

The balustrades above the Tennyson bed at Wightwick Manor are made out of turned oak, silvered with the passing of time.

FIG. I.—DWARF FENCE IN RUSTIC TRELLIS WORK.

For single gates across a carriage road, across a pathway, or anywhere else, those shown in Figs. I and 2, being of an ornamental character, will be found appropriate. The number of bars and patterns of such gates can be made to suit every purpose and gratify every taste. On carriage roads, gates should never be less than four, and seldom need be more than 6 feet in height, 5 feet being an excellent average. The construction of these gates cannot be described at length here, but the principles involved are explained by the sketches themselves, from which any carpenter of average intelligence, or any amateur who can use a saw, plane, hammer, and chisel, might easily make them. Gates may be of wood or iron as preferred. As a general

FIG. 2.—DWARF FENCE IN RUSTIC MOSAIC WORK.

pleasure ground. While they are among the most beautiful, they are certainly the most expensive of all fences. They may still be used to separate one part of the grounds from another — the rabbit-proof garden from the outside pleasure ground — where labour and expense are no object. The designs given in Figs. I and 2 are simple, but pretty, and they can be made of hazel, larch, spruce, and indeed any young trees. The bark should always be left on, and the more numerous and rougher the knots, the more rustic the fence will be. Fig. I represents a fence in rustic trellis-work. The bars of which it is formed should be slightly notched one into another at the points in which they cross, so that they may have a better bearing one against another and a firmer holding than round sticks could possibly have if nailed together without notching. For the rustic mosaic work shown in Fig. 2, sticks of hazel, maple, willow, cherry, &c., must be sawn in sunder lengthways,

rule, they should always be in harmony with the character of the fence.

Shirley Hibberd published *Rustic Adornments for Homes of Taste* in 1856 as a guide to home improvements for the middle classes. Almost every village had a carpenter or bodger who could fashion "rustic" features for the garden from the local woods.

This and following page:
Two examples of rustic work at Sunnycroft – a very simple rustic bridge over a small stream and trelliswork supporting clematis leading to the lacy screen of tamarisk.

So many ideas but where to begin? Go and find one of these three books to imbibe gardens on the cusp of Victorian and Edwardian British influences: Gertrude Jekyll and Lawrence Weaver's *Gardens for Small Country Houses* (recently republished as *The Arts and Crafts Garden*), Thomas Mawson's *Art and Craft of Garden Making*, and Edward Hudson's *Country Life* magazine.

Chapter Eight

Between a Rock and a Hard Place – Paths and Paving

The advantage of laying paths and paving is that it gives definition to the garden, in cold areas it acts as warmth storage on sunny days, and it gives you a chance to express your tastes. Narrow paths invite discovery but wide paths are more companionable and practical for wheelbarrows! People will always take the shortest route when walking to the car or compost heap so service paths need to be straight but for pleasure, create a path around the garden so that you do not have to retrace your steps. If you have a source of old materials remember that you only need one good side or edge to create a path, wall, or paving; the damaged or cracked sides are then lost in the mortar and thus not seen. Remember, the better the foundations, the safer the path but the smaller the foundation, the easier it is to change the design!

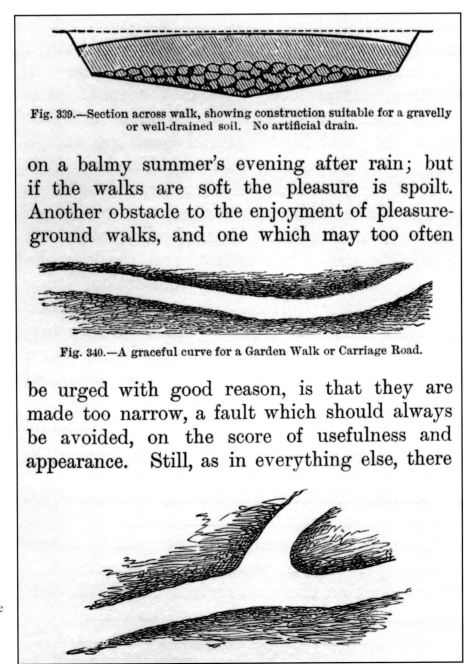

Fig. 339.—Section across walk, showing construction suitable for a gravelly or well-drained soil.   No artificial drain.

on a balmy summer's evening after rain; but if the walks are soft the pleasure is spoilt. Another obstacle to the enjoyment of pleasure-ground walks, and one which may too often

Fig. 340.—A graceful curve for a Garden Walk or Carriage Road.

be urged with good reason, is that they are made too narrow, a fault which should always be avoided, on the score of usefulness and appearance.   Still, as in everything else, there

A stroll round the garden should be companionable so try and make the path wide enough for two.

Try not to make one central path down the garden but one that leads around the garden so that you do not have to retrace your steps – note the simple brick edging.

The great paviors and walls which form the Lindisfarne Castle garden are softened by *Stachys* (Rabbits Ears).

By setting the sundial in paving it becomes a more dramatic feature in the lawn at Arley Hall.

Think about usage – an occasional garden walk versus a main thoroughfare. If you want to play around with patterns, mix up some "drylene" – one part cement to six parts sand (add one part lime if you want a paler mixture). Mix up dry and use dry as a base, then arrange your paviours, pebbles, or bricks onto the dry mixture. Finally just water them in. No sloppy cement mixture hardening and plenty of time for change.

The best way to introduce creeping plants into newly laid paving and paths is to plant them in beds alongside, then leave the plants to adventure; they will find cracks and crevices for their roots which would be impossible for you to achieve. Alternatively, seeds and small bulbs can be inserted about a year after laying, when leaching from the cement which burns young roots will have ceased.

Whether you are planning a garden shed, or a thatched summerhouse, or a pergola start at the bottom and ensure it is built on a sound base. A raft of concrete is fine if the floor is not on view. If it is, look around for decorative and utilitarian inspiration. You may not want to go the extremes of mares' teeth (I am not joking), but you can use materials such as pebbles, tiles, bricks, or even, as at Easton Lodge, a pattern of metal drain covers. We have mixed paving with setts (square small bricks), cobbles, and bricks for a textured effect. Masoned stone in the right setting provides an austere, architectural grandeur.

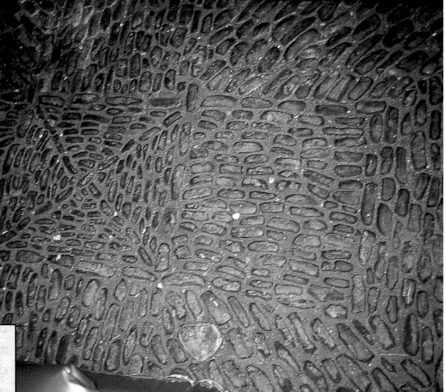

Jekyll designed the local Bargate sandstone into a hard wearing patterned floor for her summer house – this can be achieved with the good edge of broken tiles, pebbles or stones.

PERSPECTIVE VIEW OF SUMMER-HOUSE.

The home carpenter might be able to make the structure of the summerhouse but this roof, rather than trellis, would require the skills of a thatcher.

Artist, craftsman, and ever practical, Jekyll designed these small paved squares for her hydrangeas in oak barrels, pleasing the eye and easier to maintain.

The thatched summerhouse at Arts and Crafts Wightwick Manor could have been built to the sketch – tucked away in the trees it really provides a shady retreat.

A recently but traditionally built pergola – brick pillars with wooden struts and attractive brick paths inviting you to explore the gardens.

A simple iron fence and gate leaves the countryside in view but uninvited guests out.

Chapter Nine

A Drop of Water – Pools

The choice of water features, fountains, pools, and basins, as with all other aspects of Victorian gardens is vast and can be tailored to all sizes of gardens. In many of the illustrations in this book, a pool forms a focal point. It is also a mirror that enhances the buildings and creates the illusion of plants cascading from blue skies and clouds. Still water, whether a lake or on a terrace, provides the perfect canvas for water lilies which not only inspired, most famously, Monet, but poets such as Alfred, Lord Tennyson, and garden writers like William Robinson.

The illustration for a Rose Garden, designed by Leslie Greening, centers on a sculpted lily pool which encapsu-

lates both the Italianate and Arts and Crafts styles. The layout is simple and pleasing. The beds need not be confined to roses; mix in perennial herbaceous plants, bulbs, and annuals. The beds could be formally hedged with box or a haze of lavender or *Nepeta* that will help to scent the air. If space is limited and you enjoy home-grown food, introduce standard gooseberries, strawberries, and step-over espalier apples or trained grape vines. The colored chards such as rainbow and ruby or red lettuces were all popular Victorian vegetables and are easy to grow. Refer back to the Victorian Artisan's Garden for a suggested list.

The unfurling and refolding of water lilies and their nymph like appearance inspired poets and painters.

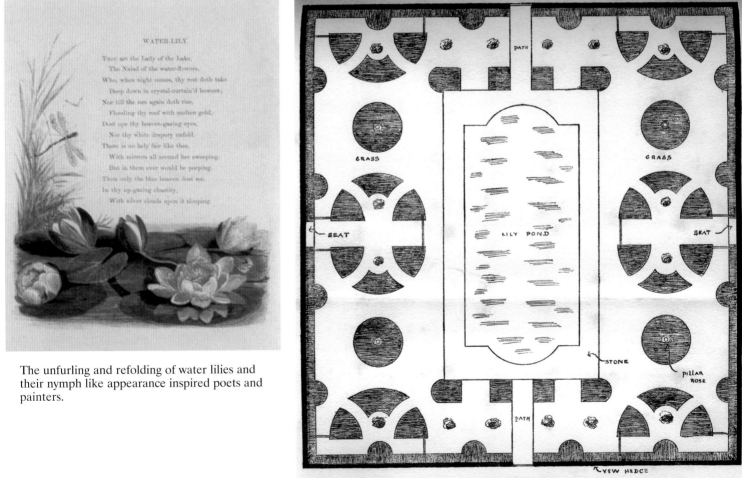

PLAN OF A ROSE GARDEN BY LESLIE GREENING.
Scale 1 inch = 15 feet.

Leslie Greening's rose garden design centered on a lily pool encapsulates both the Italianate and Arts and Crafts styles.

The sunken circular fountain at Osborne House offers a strongly formal element to this part of the garden.

Nesfield designed balustraded double steps around the water feature at Broughton Hall bringing Italianate drama into a relatively small area.

Although the Victorians did not have electrical pumps, we can combine modern technology with old fashioned designs for the drama and sound of fountains and cascades in the garden. If space permits, a pair of steps surrounding a water feature provides a dramatic exit and entrance from one part of the garden to another. At the Plantation Garden, Henry Trevor's hand-built Gothic Fountain made full use of local materials, history, and imagination – what takes time is the moss-covered ancient look. The Italian Garden at Longwood Gardens, Pennsylvania epitomizes the reverse – the decades do not show here and the effect is one of austere, architectural order.

Henry Trevor's hand-built Gothic Fountain made full use of local materials, history, and imagination

The Italian Garden at Longwood Gardens, Pennsylvania epitomizes the clean lines
water, turf, and paving can provide.

In France, Joseph Bory Latour-Marliac was the first man to hybridize European and American water lilies at his nursery at Temple sur Lot producing new colors ranging from carmine to yellow and white. His work immediately attracted the attention of William Robinson who reported the new varieties to British readers and went to see Latour-Marliac's six month display at the 1889 *Exposition Universelle* in Paris. Through the ensuing decades, water lilies were dispatched throughout France, England, Russia, and the United States. Latour-Marliac named his new varieties for his best customers such as the *Nymphaea Robinsonia* for William Robinson.

Robinson dedicated the 1893 bound edition of *The Garden* to Latour-Marliac with the words: *"To Mons. B. Latour-Marliac who has brought the colours and forms of the water lilies of the east to the waters of the north."* In 1893, Mr. L.W. Goodell of the Massachusetts Horticultural Society wrote:

> *In planting large, artificial or natural ponds, do not above all things, set the Nymphaeas in regular rows at equal distances apart, as though it were an agricultural crop needing cultivation with a horse hoe.*

Joseph Bory Latour-Marliac was the first man to hybridize water lilies (and popularize bamboos) at his nursery in Temple sur Lot and then dispatch them throughout France, England, Russia, and the United States.

Latour-Marliac's water lily tanks still exist and his nursery still supplies the world with water lilies.

The first of three pools in New Orleans gardens: a grand architectural statement that allows you to sit and dip your hands in the cooling water.

Victorian style water features remain the classical choice as can be seen in the photographs of three contemporary pools in New Orleans gardens. Water is an essential in summer gardens not just for the human occupants but for birds whose dipping actions are a constant source of pleasure. In a small garden, the ideas that Henry Trevor used for the Gothic Fountain can be scaled down to provide a small pool, a display area for containers, a place to sit and dip your fingers in the water as well as grow water lilies, and perhaps keep fish. Water provides a veritable cornucopia of Victorian hobbies in just one feature!

A sunken pool whose well-like depths draw the eye, brightened by seasonal pots in a Moorish style.

A shady corner that maximizes the potential for interest – quadripartite beds, statues. and dish fountain.

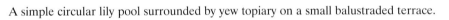

A simple circular lily pool surrounded by yew topiary on a small balustraded terrace.

Harold Peto designed this magnificent Italianate pool for Daisy, Countess of Warwick in 1903. Latour-Marliac nurseries supplied the water lilies.

Nymphaea Escarboule on the restored pool at Easton Lodge, formerly Warwick House in Essex.

The terrace with lily pool Lutyens designed for Jekyll at Munstead Wood incorporates their love of steps and local materials.

Jekyll and Monet both bought water lilies from Latour-Marliac. Jekyll bought five franc varieties whilst Monet purchased twenty franc water lilies.

Latour-Marliac's water lilies were featured in many magazines and catalogues, tempting gardeners to paint their pools with bright colors.

A modern and exuberant interpretation of the raised wall lily pool.

Chapter Ten

A Walk in a Victorian Rose Garden

An English rose is a term used to describe classic female beauty; the English rose garden was created by homesick patriots serving in all parts of the extensive Victorian British Empire. Formal rose gardens can still be seen under tropical, arid, or temperate skies from India to Africa to Australia. Rose gardens can be so much more than just roses. Many new varieties in the mid nineteenth century lacked scent, fuelling a revival of interest in old roses and experiments with introducing new scented varieties. Victorian clergymen are associated with enthusiastic rose growing. Dean Hole who wrote *A Book about Roses* and the Reverend Pemberton who bred Hybrid Musk roses such as Cornelia, Felicia, and Penelope are just two of many. Roses seem to express leisure and love, beautifully captured in John Boyle O'Reilly's poem *A White Rose:*

> *The red rose whispers of passion,*
> *And the white rose breathes of love;*
> *O, the red rose is a falcon,*
> *And the white rose is a dove.*
> *But I send you a cream-white rosebud*
> *With a flush on its petal tips;*
> *For the love that is purest and sweetest*
> *Has a kiss of desire on the lips.*

WHERE THE PERFUME OF THE ROSE IS SWEETEST.

> *How well the skilful gardener drew*
> *Of flowers, and herbs, this dial new,*
> *Where, from above, the milder sun*
> *Does through a fragrant zodiac run,*
> *And, as it works, the industrious bee*
> *Computes its tune as well as we!*
> *How could such sweet and wholesome hours*
> *Be reckoned but with herbs and flowers?*
> —Andrew Marvell, *Thoughts in a Garden*

Beatrice Parsons entitled her illustration for Roses and Rose Gardens "Ramblers and Bush Roses in an Old-World Garden."

Beatrice Parsons paints roses in an exuberant and natural setting – the heady scents of summer, the buzz of bees, and a rambling garden. In compact gardens it is worth considering a plan; the small Victorian plan illustrated gives you somewhere to wander and even to sit. In a little area like this, complement the Victorian roses with herbs such as thymes, lavender, and rosemary that enjoyed a revival at that time. A framework of fine iron, wood, or rope invites either the formality of climbing roses or the informality of rambling roses. Standard roses were introduced in the late nineteenth century. Nurseryman will still bud to order so if you want a traditional taller standard, say, six feet tall, inquire before buying the customary modern four feet standards. Stocks budded with climbing roses will make ordinary standards, those with rambling roses, weeping standards.

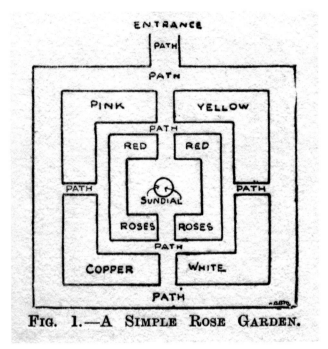

FIG. 1.—A SIMPLE ROSE GARDEN.

Very simple but with nothing to look at in the winter so include bulbs for winter and spring and herbs.

The iron framework in the Pond Garden at Audley End with trained rambling roses offers a window out and into the rose garden.

The Rose Garden at Tatton Park in Cheshire is enclosed away from the main gardens. The design is a simple sun ray effect lined with a pergola. The other half of the garden has a small stone bathing pool. The shapes and styles here can be decanted for the smaller garden – remember one large bed is more effective than a series of small fussy shapes. A statue or water feature can make an excellent centerpiece or training roses into a maypole such as the one illustrated at Wightwick Manor. This is well described in Beeton's *Shilling Gardener:*

Beds, Tent - These are formed by the aid of chains, flexible wires, or ropes. Drive a tall stake of the desired height, say 10 feet high, in the centre; describe a circle with a radius of, say, 8 feet. Insert six or eight stakes at equal distances on this line, say 6 feet high; join the centre stake to each side one with a chain or wire, and the frame of a tent bed is formed.

The Rose Garden at Tatton Park was designed with radiating beds surrounded by a pergola supporting climbing and rambling roses. Narrow paths make access easy.

The Rose Garden at Tatton Park in high summer at its traditional Victorian best.

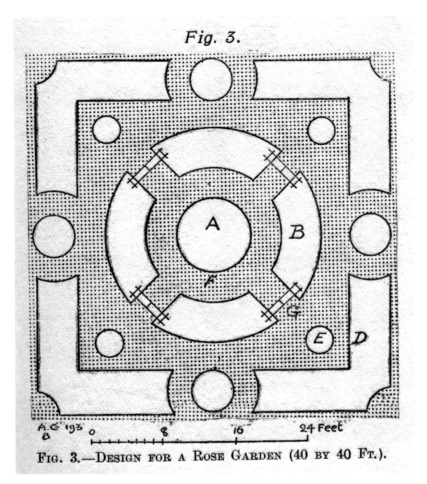

Fig. 3.

FIG. 3.—DESIGN FOR A ROSE GARDEN (40 BY 40 FT.).

The center piece of this Rose Garden could take several forms
and the use of squares and circles gives it more movement.

The roses have been trained like Beeton's tent bed or a maypole in the center of the rose garden at
Wightwick Manor. The central pole makes a perfect spot to sit and enjoy the musk of the roses.

A delightful central wirework arbor like the one at Waddesdon Manor would be a major investment but with the advantage of year round appeal and it should hold its value. Another Rothschild garden surrounds the Villa Ephrussi de Rothschild at Cap Ferrat, France. Baroness Beatrice de Rothschild, by marriage Mme Ephrussi, created gardens like the deck of a cruise ship. The house looks out onto a formal French garden in *creole* style with sentinel palm trees and agaves terminating in a copy of the Trianon's Temple d'Amour. Other gardens include Spanish, Japanese, English, and Provençal gardens, a Florentine terrace, Lapidary garden and a *jardin exotique* of steep winding paths around impressive cactii. The west facing rosary is laid out in formal box edged beds terraced in a fan from a white colonnade and temple with climbers and faience pots of Santolina, in every sense the high point of this voluptuous rose garden with its dramatic views across the Mediterranean.

A delightful central wirework arbor would be a major investment but has year round appeal.

The rose garden at Villa Ephrussi de Rothschild is west facing on a gentle slope, the planting is terraced with each flowerbed box-edged. The garden is topped by a white colonnade and temple – in every sense the high point of this voluptuous rose garden with its dramatic views across the Mediterranean.

Northern Europe is not noted for endless sunshine and blue skies but in compensation, Dutch nurseries have produced brightly colored plants for centuries. The Victorian plan for a Dutch style rose garden is designed for a flat site, however, if you have a sloping site you could adapt the paths into staggered terraces such as the Ephrussi garden. Even if the steps were shallow it would make more impact and you could use the cracks and crevices for creeping plants.

Although the Dutch style is designed for a flat site, the paths could be adapted to steps for a sloping site to very good effect.

FIG. 6.—ROSE GARDEN IN DUTCH STYLE.

If you have a Victorian style rose garden near you it is worth visiting in winter to note how they train and prune their roses. The illustration of the Victorian rose garden at Warwick Castle in winter gives you the opportunity to appreciate the delicate ironwork encircling the roses and the way the standards have been trained.

Although the Dorothy Perkins rose was not introduced until 1902, its small pink cluster flowers lend themselves to cottage gardens. Sadly Dorothy Perkins is prone to mildew but fares much better when allowed to scramble through yew hedges as can be seen in the illustration of our gate. E.R. Rowe's Edwardian illustration of "Dorothy Perkins over trellis work" epitomizes Arts and Crafts rose growing' the trellis is hardly visible, the bulbous terracotta amphorae gently bringing the raised bed in and out of focus. Presumably the doves in the dovecote behind would provide a gentle background sound of billing and cooing. Many nineteenth century rambling roses will grow up a tree (ideal for the smaller garden) or a large tree stump such as the rich Tea scented Alister Stella Gray pictured here. Alister Stella Gray was introduced in 1894 and has blooms that are yellow paling to creamy-white. Edward Cooke's idea of a stumpery at Biddulph Grange became very fashionable; an alternative for those not wishing to uproot dead trees was simply to use them as an informal support for rambling roses.

On this and following page:
The Victorian rose garden at Warwick Castle in winter. Note the delicate ironwork encircling the roses and, below, each bed with low clipped box hedging. The standards are carefully trained to provide balanced shapes in summer.

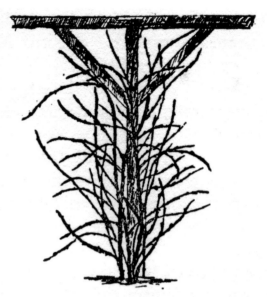

A PILLAR ROSE BEFORE PRUNING IN SPRING.

A PILLAR ROSE AFTER PRUNING.
The old canes have been cut out, and the new ones tied up.

At present this tree looks stiff, but by June it will be a mass of loose, graceful growth and bloom.

Other views of the Victorian rose garden

Good diagrammatic advice from a Victorian rose book on how to prune your pillar roses – today we would advise pruning from December to March depending on your zone.

E.R. Rowe's illustration *Dorothy Perkins over trellis work* epitomizes Arts and Crafts rose growing – the trellis is hardly visible, the bulbous terracotta amphorae gently bringing the raised bed in and out of focus. Presumably the doves in the dovecote behind would provide a gentle background sound of billing and cooing.

The rose Dorothy Perkins cascades down our hedge in Suffolk – it seems to suffer less from mildew in this situation than over an ironwork trellis.

Many nineteenth century rambling roses will grow up a tree (ideal for the smaller garden) or a large tree stump such as the rich tea scented Alister Stella Gray, introduced in 1894, pictured here. The blooms are yellow paling to creamy-white.

ROSES GROUPED ON ROUGH STUMPS.
Fellenberg, the Dawson, and the Wichuraianas make beautiful clumps when grown in this way.

Stumperies were a Victorian feature – upturned dead trees whose roots provide pockets and niches for small plants or an informal framework for roses.

The final Victorian illustration of the traditional rose garden at Shiplake is simple, easy to maintain, and has a style still emulated the world over. Wyck in Philadelphia was the home to nine generations of the Quaker Wistar and Haines families, still surrounded by a two and one-half acre garden whose rose garden echoes Shiplake in style and its collection of old nineteenth century roses.

A farewell view down a traditional Victorian rose garden with symmetrically arranged beds all neatly hedged in dwarf box, a style still emulated the world over.

ROSE GARDEN AT SHIPLAKE COURT.
Here Box edging is used to divide the beds from the lawn in the Formal Garden.

Chapter Eleven

Finishing Touches — Topiary, Espalier, and Fernery

This final chapter summarizes three gardening skills that have appeared at various points in the book. Trained plants give year round interest and architectural form to the garden as well as privacy. If you wait until the vigorous flush of growth is over in early summer, topiary only needs clipping once or twice a year. You can buy ready trained espalier and fan trained fruits and shrubs which just require common sense and judicious pruning twice a year as well. Ferns are another matter but can be grown in the house, greenhouse, or garden, and encapsulate the Victorian quest for knowledge and self-improvement.

A yew enclosed green topiary garden set in diamonds of stone and turf. Early morning frost gives a magical quality to the arrangement. In summer, the greens are refreshingly quiet. The good news is that yew topiary only needs clipping once or twice a year.

Hunting scenes, animals, birds, and humor are all clipped into the topiaries that fill the grounds of Ladew Topiary Garden in Maryland.

In the hands of a clever clipper you can have an aviary or menagerie in your garden. The peacock offers elegance and draws the eye towards the clipped arch at the end of the walk at Wightwick Manor.

Jan Greenland clipped this cat in her shrubbery in one afternoon as a joke for her children, ten years later the humor remains!

Topiary expresses the garden's personality: immaculate shaped formality (try and see the awesome exhibits at the Philadelphia Flower Show) or skilled shaping of animals, birds, airplanes, pianos, etc. The peacock illustrated offers elegance and draws the eye towards the clipped arch at the end of the walk at Wightwick Manor. What the cat is doing in Jan Greenland's topiary in her shrubbery is open to speculation but it is such fun that it makes you smile every time you leave the front door. You might wish to create a chess set or one of the Egyptian pyramids like Biddulph Grange. Today you can buy wire frames to fit over the embryo evergreens to help you shape up. The Victorians also trained ivy into baskets, animals, and around topiaries.

White paint and polished brass make a perfect Victorian backdrop for these green and white planters in New Orleans – choose an evergreen to suit your climate and underplant accordingly.

Stepping down past the agapanthus to the avenue of Portuguese laurel (*Prunus lusitanica*) that lines the walk behind Fenton House in London. Portuguese laurel is a good substitute for sweet bay (*Laurus nobilis*) in colder areas.

If you have an overgrown or damaged yew in your garden, help is at hand; yews will grow vigorously from old wood. Never cut back more than one third of a yew and when drastically cutting back, mulch the roots over-winter to feed it. In three years you can have a completely rejuvenated yew. Yew is much less invasive than people imagine and makes a perfect dark backdrop for flowers or even for you and your guests when elegantly dressed in silks and satins.

The gardens of Villandry have numerous yew topiaries: look carefully for the good news – if for any reason you lose part of yew topiary or if it becomes very overgrown, yew will reshoot from the trunk so all is never lost.

In the days when you could not pop down to the supermarket to buy fruit, no wall space was wasted that might produce plums, pears, peaches, or apples. Take a leaf out of the Victorian fruit books and use all available wall surfaces including your house— imagine the pleasure of picking fresh fruit from your bedroom window.

However, Andrew Downing advised that *"Such a thing as a wall for fruit trees, in a cottage garden, is nearly unknown in the United States, and therefore we need say nothing respecting training them to a wall."* He recommended a Bartlett, a Seckel, and a Dutchess (sic) of Angouleme Pear; George the Fourth, and a Yellow Rareripe Peach; Imperial Gage and Golden Drop Plum; Mayduke, and a Downer's Late Red Cherry; and a Moorpark Apricot with strawberries growing beneath to be planted along outer borders.

Take a note out of the Victorian fruit books, use all available wall surfaces including your house. Imagine the pleasure of picking fresh fruit from your bedroom window.

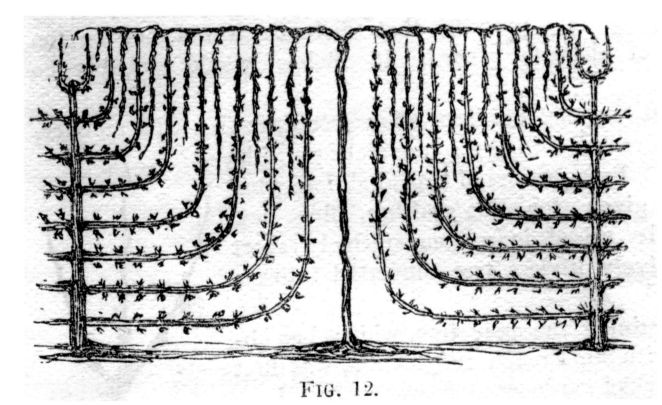

FIG. 12.

An espaliered pear and grape vine, hopefully as fruitful as ornamental. The vine is trained, as the Romans did, to create a hanging curtain.

The demonstration fruit garden at the Chicago Botanical Garden has inspirational espalier fruit training. In winter, training to this complexity can be used as an architectural feature or ornate screen. At West Dean, near Chichester in Sussex, the wealthy James family entertained the Prince of Wales, later Edward VII. In recent years the Victorian and Edwardian kitchen gardens have been restored to demonstrate traditional methods of growing vegetables and raising fruit. The apple tree illustrated is being trained into a "goblet," leaving the center open for air circulation and ripening not to mention ease of picking.

The demonstration fruit garden at the Chicago Botanical Garden has inspirational espalier fruit training. In winter, training to this complexity can be used as an architectural feature or ornate screen.

Victorian and Edwardian methods of growing vegetables and raising fruit are demonstrated in the gardens at West Dean. The apple tree here is being trained into a "goblet," leaving the center open for air circulation and ripening.

An untrained Lord Derby apple in blossom – a spring pleasure with promises for the future. In the language of flowers, to present a loved one with apple blossom shows preference – what greater preferential treatment than giving part of the possible future harvest.

One of the most important nurseries in England was Rivers of Sawbridgeworth. Thomas Rivers designed and popularized the idea of an orchard house where top and soft fruit trees and bushes were raised in pots. Methods that can be easily adapted for the modern small garden. The epitome of the gardener's art were potted vines for the dinner table; guests literally harvested their fresh grapes from the vine.

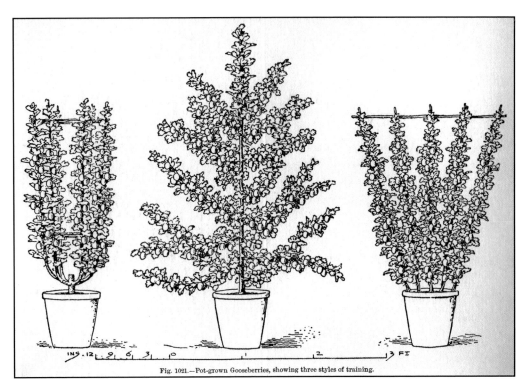

Fig. 1021.—Pot-grown Gooseberries, showing three styles of training.

Thomas Rivers designed and popularized the idea of an orchard house and raising top and soft fruit trees and bushes in pots – methods that can be easily adapted for the modern small garden. The epitome of the gardener's art was potted vines for the dinner table; guests literally harvested their fresh grapes from the vine.

The Aesthetic Room at the Geffrye Museum of Domestic Interiors provides a bounteous harvest of plant ideas. Look at nineteenth century wallpapers, tiles, glass, and ceramics for tree, shrub, and plant ideas. Don't forget the Victorian tip of putting a large mirror on the wall opposite your windows; it lightens the room and brings the garden indoors. Then pull up a chair, get out the books, and start dreaming and scheming. Andrew Downing advised planting scented shrubs like *Daphne mezereum, Calycanthus florida, Rosa champneyana, Celthra alnifolia, Magnolia obovata* and *Ribes aureum* under the windows of your "cottage" so that their fragrance might be enjoyed throughout the house.

The Aesthetic Room at the Geffrye Museum of Domestic Interiors in London provides a bounteous harvest of plant ideas. Look at nineteenth century wallpapers, tiles, glass, and ceramics for tree, shrub, and plant ideas. Don't forget the Victorian tip of putting a large mirror on the wall opposite your windows; it lightens the room and brings the garden indoors. Then pull up a chair, get out the books and start dreaming and scheming.

Shady Greens – Ferns

The fern craze was enjoyed by all classes and all pockets, the humbler collector seeking local varieties, the wealthy funding worldwide hunts. The plan illustrated relates to the restored fernery at Eschott Hall in Northumberland. The stones of the fernery in spring are softened by moss with highlights of rhododendrons under the deciduous trees. The addition of the Tree Fern (*Dicksonia*) into this restoration mirrors the Victorian fascination with this rootless Australian introduction. The summer sunshine is filtered by the surrounding trees to provide a dappled shade as you wend your way around the fernery. The play of light through the foliage and onto the ferns makes you feel you are approaching the dawn of time. Inside or out, large or small, there was a huge choice of adornments and paraphernalia to enliven ferneries. If space is limited it is better to collect one or two species of ferns that enjoy the same conditions rather than juggling the needs of a wider variety.

The fern craze was enjoyed by all classes and all pockets – the humbler collector seeking local varieties, the wealthy funding worldwide hunts. This plan relates to the restored fernery at Eschott Hall in Northumberland.

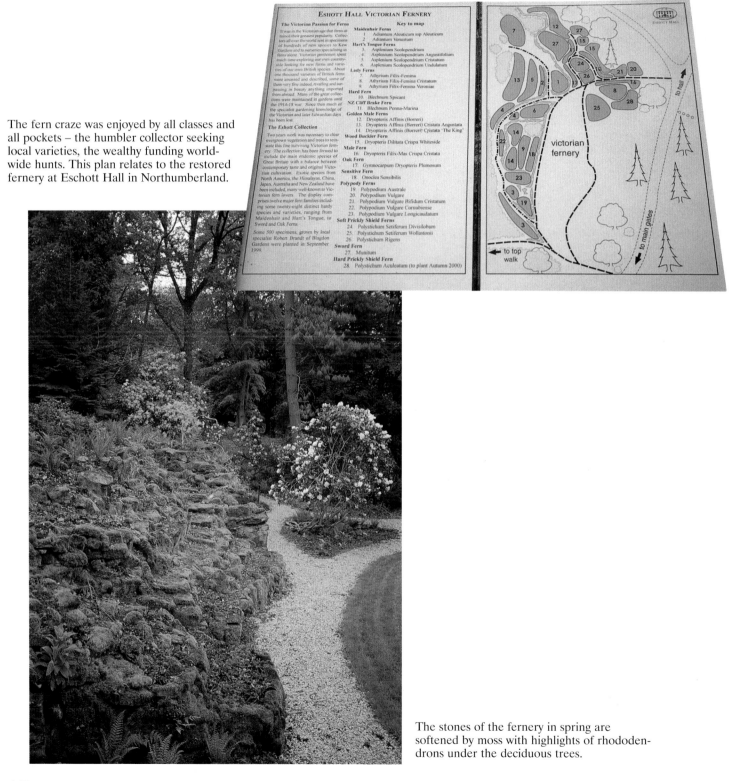

The stones of the fernery in spring are softened by moss with highlights of rhododendrons under the deciduous trees.

148

As the summer sets in, the surrounding trees provide a dappled shade as you wend your way around the fernery.

The play of light through the foliage and onto the leaves makes you feel you are approaching the dawn of time.

Shirley Hibberd placed the fernery in the "truly rustic" rather than "rural" department of gardening and then proceeds to describe in great detail how to make artificial rockwork for ferns! The ideal soil was *"a foundation of sandy loam, old lime, and brick rubbish, and afterwards made up with a compost of two parts of heath-mould, two of rotten leaves, and one of potsherds or flower-pots broken into small pieces."* Very much in the spirit of Biddulph Grange, he also writes about how he had piled up dead tree roots *in no particular order* to form a primitive arbor weaving their roots into a roof around and on to which he

…piled up a mass of rotten wood and moss, which had been collected for cultural purposes…so as to construct a sort of extemporaneous hermit's cell, or grotto of wood…among the roots, on the ground, and on the bank of rubbish at the back,… planted spare ferns…the ferns flourished, and a number of pretty wildings sprung up from the moss…one of the prettiest Ferneries…ever seen.

Inside or out, large or small, there was a huge choice of adornments and paraphernalia to enliven ferneries.

150

A thatched summer house or seat provides a more sophisticated *natural* place to sit and admire your gardening labors. The thatch around the tree above the garden seat adjusts as the tree thickens, fun with the appearance of a large mushroom!

A natural place to sit and admire your gardening labors; the thatch adjusts as the tree thickens.

151

The creation of Victorian elements in a garden must include time to just sit and stare; indeed use the ideas to make your life more leisurely. You may not have a gardener but modern technology can help you cheat in speeding up traditional methods. In America, the social goal was to have every man own his own home. Andrew Downing's quest was to foster the belief that just one perfectly grown tree in a lawn with surrounding flowers and shrubs achieved the "beautiful" garden.

In conclusion, Sam Beeton, in pompous Victorian prose said:

The love of gardening among Englishmen and Scotchmen, too, is steadily on the increase, and has been so for a long series of years; and therefore the demand for such handbooks as these in which gardening as it ought to be done is described briefly but tersely, and in a manner which the lowest capacity ought to be able to grasp and assimilate.

No one should feel that their gardening skills are of the "lowest capacity" – modest perhaps. Have fun weaving eclectic and beautiful Victorian ideas back into gardens, yards, and window boxes.

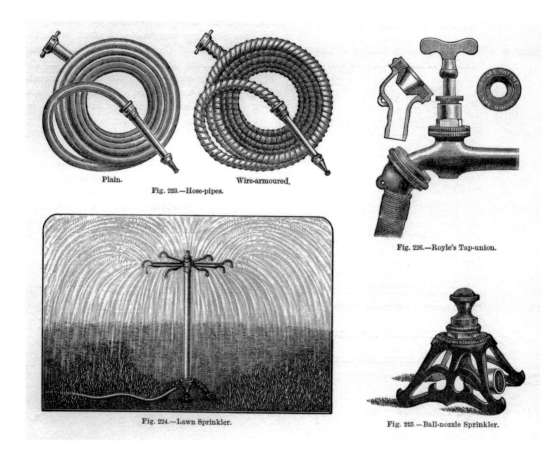

Plain.　　Wire-armoured.

Fig. 223.—Hose-pipes.

Fig. 224.—Lawn Sprinkler.

Fig. 226.—Royle's Tap-union.

Fig. 225.—Ball-nozzle Sprinkler.

The following are brief biographies of people whose names have been mentioned in the text or, if you have an active interest in Victorian garden history, that you might want to investigate further. The list is by no means exhaustive but should lead the reader down some interesting garden paths.

Queen Victoria **(1819-1901)**

Reigned 1837-1901. Married to Prince Albert Saxe-Coburg-Gotha. Royal residences include Buckingham Palace, Windsor Castle, and Osborne House; in Scotland, Holyrood Palace, Balmoral. Gave Sandringham House as wedding present to son Edward (VII).

Barry, Sir Charles **(1795-1860)**

Architect of the Houses of Parliament. Designed Italianate gardens at Trentham (intricate parterres designed by George Fleming (1809-1876), Dunrobin Castle, Kiddington, Gawthorpe Hall, Shrubland Park, Harewood House, Cliveden (worked with head gardener, John Fleming, son of George and innovator of carpet bedding).

Bateman, James **(1811-1897)**

Orchids were the master passion of his life. Published *Orchidaecea of Mexico and Guatemala*. Married Maria Egerton-Warburton (knowledgeable on herbaceous plants, fuchsias, and lilies). Bought Biddulph Grange in 1840 creating a world of gardens. Helped and recorded by watercolorist E.W. Cooke.

Blomfield, Sir Reginald **(1856-1942)**

Architect, garden designer (including. Godinton, Kent; Mellerstain, Borders; Brocklesby, Lincs; Caythorpe, Lincs) and author of *The Formal Garden in England* (1892). Very vociferous in late Victorian and Edwardian formal garden design. Contemporary and vitriolic opponent of **William Robinson.**

Downing, Andrew Jackson **(1815-1852)**

Son of a nurseryman. American garden architect and author of *A Treatise on the Theory and Practice of Landscape Gardening* (1841), and *Cottage Residences* (1842). Many times reprinted and widely influential in popularizing the beautiful and picturesque into the smallest gardens. Inspired Frederick Law Olmsted.

Fortune, Robert **(1812-80)**

Scottish plant collector. First into China after Opium Wars of 1842, made several expeditions into China funded both by the Horticultural Society and the East India Company. Introduced "Japanese" anemones, chrysanthemums, *Dicentra*, winter jasmine, forsythia, weigela, winter honeysuckle. Also noted for sending tea plants from China to Kew for introduction into India, similarly *Actinidia* or Chinese gooseberries into New Zealand (now better known as the kiwi fruit.)

Gray, Professor Asa **(1810-1888)**

Distinguished American botanist, Professor of Natural History at Harvard, 1842-1888, author with John Torrey of *Flora of North America* (1838-43). One of founding fathers of Arnold Arboretum.

Hibberd, Shirley **(1825-1890)**

Born in Stepney, lived in Stoke Newington. Popular Victorian gardening author; studied problems of urban and suburban horticulture; authored *Rustic Adornment for Homes of Taste* (1856), *Brambles and Bay*, and *The Town Garden*.

Hole, Rev. Samuel Reynolds **(1819-1904)**

Dean of Rochester, first President of the Royal National Rose Society; author of *A Book about Roses* and *A Book about the Garden*.

Hooker, Sir William Jackson **(1785-1865)**

Born in Norwich; 1820-1841– Chair of Botany at Glasgow based at eight acre University Botanical Gardens, Sandyford (9,000 species on his arrival 12,000 by 1825); 1827-1865 Author and editor of *Curtis' Botanical Magazine*; knighted in 1839; appointed first (paid) Director of Kew in1841.

Hooker, Sir Joseph Dalton **(1817-1911)**

Born Halesworth son of Sir William; educated Glasgow; 1839-1843 HMS Erebus voyage to the Antarctic, South America, Australia, New Zealand, and South Africa; lasting friendship with Charles Darwin (1809-1882) finally accepting his theories; 1847 elected to Royal Society; received Treasury grant to collect plants for Kew from Sikkim, Eastern Himalayas. Discovered twenty-six species of rhododendron in one day; 1850 plant hunting in Khasi Mountains (with Thomas Thomson); 1855 appointed Deputy Director at Kew; 1860 studied Cedar of Lebanon groves in Palestine and Syria (with Daniel Hanbury); 1865 Director of Kew; 1865-1904 Editor of *Botanical Magazine*; 1867 edited *Hooker's Icones Plantarum*; 1871 plant hunting in Morocco (with John Ball and George Maw); 1873-78 President of the Royal Society; 1877 knighted; 1877 phytogeographical expedition to Colorado, Utah, and Sierra Nevada; 1885 retired.

Jekyll, Gertrude (1843-1932)

Trained as an artist (exhibited at the Royal Academy in 1865) whose failing sight directed her towards gardening and writing. Her sense of color and form with horticultural insight and knowledge made a formidable combination. Influenced by **William Robinson** and worked with Edwin Lutyens. Lived in The Hut whilst she created the gardens of Munstead Wood from 1883. Jekyll was an excellent photographer which has provided accurate records of the gardens and plants. Published her first book in 1899 *Wood and Garden*.

Latour-Marliac, Joseph Bory (1830-1911)

Staged six month display of his new hybrid water lilies, received three gold medals 1889 at Exposition Universelle, Paris. Nursery still in existence at Temple sur Lot, France

Lindley, Dr. John (1799-1865)

Worked with Joseph Banks in founding the Horticultural Society of London (now the RHS). Led enquiry into role of the Royal Gardens at Kew with Joseph Paxton that resulted in its opening to the public in 1841. Edited *The Gardeners Chronicle*. Received and attributed many new introductions; Wrote *The Theory and Practice of Horticulture* (1840), and *The Vegetable Kingdom* (1846).

Monet, Claude (1840-1926)

Impressionists took their name from his *L'impression: soleil levant*. Moved to final house in Giverny in 1883, bought the adjoining water meadow in 1893 to create pond gardens. Fine collections of Japanese plants, irises, roses, water lilies often working with Jardin des Plantes, Paris.

Morris, William (1834-96)

English poet, artist, craftsman, decorator, and social reformer. Friend Philip Webb built the Red House, Bexley Heath for him and his wife Jane. Rose trellis inspired one of the first fabrics produced by Morris, Marshal, Faulkner & Co. Prime mover in the Arts and Crafts Movement with it sociological and aesthetic aims i.e. Kelmscott Manor. Garden sentiments and dislike of over-artificiality in flowers shared by **William Robinson** and Forbes Watson.

Nesfield, William Andrews (1793-1881)

Ex Army officer and watercolorist, designed large parts of Kew, Horticultural Society Gardens at Kensington, Broughton Hall, Castle Howard, Holme Pierrepont Hall, Holkham, Somerleyton, Witley Court. Renowned for his intricate parterres and grand fountains. Later worked in partnership with his sons, William Eden (1835-1888) and Markham (c.1842-1874).

Olmsted, Frederick Law (1822-1903)

America's first landscape architect and city planner (Arnold Arboretum). Designed with Calvert Vaux New York's Central Park. Instigator of National Parks, consultant and designer of many city parks (Boston, Berkeley, Chicago, Cincinnati, plus others).

Paxton, Sir Joseph (1803-65)

Trained under Lindley at Horticultural Society gardens at Chiswick. Head Gardener then agent at Chatsworth. Raised first *Victoria amazonica* on which he based his design for the Crystal Palace 1851. Lead enquiry with **Lindley** on Kew. Founder of *The Gardener's Chronicle* 1841. MP for Coventry (Coventry cemetery).

Pulham, James (1820-98) & Sons

Founded one of the earliest professional rockwork firms at Broxbourne, Herts. Devised a highly successful artificial stone "Pulhamite." Created cliffs, waterfalls, rocky stream, rocky pathways and a cave at Sandringham for Edward VII.

Robinson, William (1838-1935)

Traveled and observed in France and USA, prolific writer. Founded "The Garden." Owned and gardened Gravetye Manor from 1885. Believed a garden should grow out of its own site, great advocate of native plants, using local materials such as rustic work bridges and furniture, stone seats. and brick trellises. Vitriolic exchanges with **Blomfield** over the death note of the pastry cook's garden. Head gardener Ernest Markham. Alfred Parsons, Mark Fisher, H.A. Olivier, and H.G. Moon all painted at Gravetye. Friends with Burne-Jones and Ruskin.

Trevor, Henry (1819-1897)

Epitomizes the industrious middle class Victorian, born in Wisbech, Cambridgeshire. Trevor married his boss Joseph Gray's widowed daughter in 1843; of their four children only Eliza survived. Lived over the shop in Post-Office Street, Norwich. In 1855 leased ancient chalk quarry for seventy-five years intending to create on the three acres "beautiful and picturesque" grounds. In 1856, Trevor built a austere solid house, aptly named "The Plantation," with a smaller dwelling for his gardener and family. He lived and worked on the gardens here until his death in 1897. In 1890 White's Norfolk Directory recorded *"The Plantation...the grounds of H. Trevor Esq., situated in a deep dell, the site of ancient and extensive chalk pits, is a gem of landscape gardening, and its tropical and sub tropical collections are in high repute."*

United Kingdom

The Victorian Gate & Seating Co.
Hascoll's Farm, Lower Durston, Taunton
Somerset TA3 5AH

Andrew Raffle
Raffles Thatched Garden Buildings
Laundry Cottage
Prestwold Hall, Prestwold
Loughborough LE12 5SQ

Cast Iron Shop
394, Caledonian Road
London N1 1DW

Salvo (Salvaged and antique garden statuary and artifacts)
www.salvoweb.com

Stonemarket Ltd.
Oxford Road
Coventry CV8 3EJ

United States of America

Carolina Lanterns and Accessories
401, W. Coleman Boulevard,
Ste E, Mount Pleasant,
South Carolina
www.charlestongateway.com

Dalton Pavilions, Inc
www.daltonpavilions.com

Fine Garden Products
www.finegardenproducts.com

Gardensheds,
651, Millcross Road,
Lancaster PA17601
www.gardensheds.com/gardensheds

Ashley Powell - Tree hut frame and thatching
1 Creek Road
Christiana, PA 17509

Walpole Woodworkers
www.walpolewoodworkers.com

United Kingdom

Many properties open in late March and close in early November. Winter openings are usually shorter.

Alton Towers
Alton
Staffordshire ST10 4DB

Audley End House and Gardens
Saffron Walden
Essex CB11 4JF

Brogdale Horticultural Trust
Brogdale Road
Faversham, Kent ME13 8XZ

Drummond Castle
Muthill
Crieff PH74HZ, Tayside, Scotland
www.drummondcastlegardens.co.uk

Geffrye Museum
Kingsland Road
London E2 8EA
www.geffrye-museum.org.uk

HDRA Yalding Organic Gardens
Benover Road, Yalding
Maidstone, Kent ME18 6EX
www.hdra.org.uk

Museum of Garden History
St. Mary at Lambeth
Lambeth Palace Road
London SE1 7LB.
www.museumgardenhistory.org

Plantation Garden
Earlham Road
Norwich

Royal Botanic Gardens
Kew
Richmond TW9 3AB
www.rbgkew.org.uk

The National Trust

The National Trust (www.nationaltrust.org.uk) and the National Trust for Scotland looks after a stunning variety of properties (including Biddulph Grange, Cragside, Sunnycroft, Waddesdon Manor and Wightwick Manor) in the United Kingdom including gardens, countryside, coastline and historic properties. The Royal Oak Foundation (www.royal-oak.org) is a not-for-profit organization that helps the National Trust.

The Royal Oak Foundation
26 Broadway, Suite 950
New York, NY 10004
email general@royal-oak.org
www.royal-oak.org

Biddulph Grange Garden
Biddulph
Stoke-on-Trent ST8 7SD
Email: biddulphgrange@ntrust.org.uk

Cragside
Rothbury
Morpeth NE65 7PX
Email cragside@ntrust.org.uk

Sunnycroft
200 Holyhead Road
Wellington
Telford TF1 2DR

Waddesdon Manor
Waddesdon
email waddesdonmanor@ntrust.org.uk
www.waddesdon.org.uk

Wightwick Manor
Wolverhampton WV6 8EE
Email: wightwickmanor@ntrust.org.uk

United States of America

Arnold Arboretum
125 Arbor Way
Jamaica Plain, MA 12130
www.arboretum.harvard.edu
The arboretum developed in 1872, by Charles Sprague Sargent and Frederick Law Olmsted, created an "emerald necklace" of parks around Boston.

Charleston Festival of Houses and Gardens
Historic Charleston Foundation
PO Box 1120, Charleston, SC 29402
www.historiccharleston.org

Hagley Museum and Library
Route 141
Wilmington DE 19807
www.hagley.lib.de.us

Landmark Society House & Garden Tour
The Landmark Society of New York
133 South Fitzhugh Street
Rochester, NY 14608
Annual gardens tour of 19th & 20th century homes and gardens early June

Longwood Gardens
Route 1, PO Box 501
Kennett Square, PA 19348-0501
www.longwoodgardens.org

The Crook House Victorian Heirloom Garden
5730 North 30th Street #11B
Fort Omaha (now the campus of Metropolitan Community College)
Omaha, NE 68111-1657

The Ebenezer Maxwell Mansion Victorian Gardens
200 West Tulpehocken Street
Philadelphia PA19144

Rockwood Museum
610 Shipley Road
Wilmington DE 19809

Wyck Historic House and Gardens
6026 Germantown Avenue
Philadelphia PA 19144
www.wyck.org

United Kingdom

Craven's Nursery
1, Foulds Terrace
Bingley
West Yorkshire BD16 4LZ
Auricula, Primula, Pinks, Alpines and specialist seeds

David Austin Roses Ltd.
Bowling Green Lane
Albrighton
Wolverhampton WV7 3HB
Roses, Iris, Paeony, Hemerocallis
www.davidaustinroses.com

HDRA - The Organic Organization
Heritage Seed Library
Ryton Organic Gardens
Coventry CV8 3LG.
Heritage seed distributed to members
www.hdra.org.uk

Kelways Ltd.
Langport
Somerset TA10 9EZ
Paeony, Iris, Hemerocallis, Herbaceous perennials
www.kelways.com

Michael Paske Farms Ltd.
Estate Office
Honington
Grantham
Lincolnshire NG32 2PG
Sea kale thongs, asparagus crowns and seeds, artichokes
paske.farms@farmline.com

Mr. Fothergill's Seeds Ltd.
Gazeley Road
Kentford
Newmarket
Suffolk CB8 8QB
Flowers and vegetables
www.mr-fothergills.co.uk

Reads Nursery
Hales Hall
Loddon
Norfolk NR14 6QW.
Conservatory, citrus, figs, fruits and nuts, wall shrubs, scented and aromatic, topiary
www.readsnursery.co.uk

W. Robinson & Sons Ltd.
Sunny Bank
Forton
Preston
Lancashire PR3 0BN.
Specialist giant and exhibition vegetable seed
www.mammothonion.co.uk

The Romantic Garden
Swannington
Norwich NR9 5NW
Half hardy & Conservatory, Buxus topiary, Ornamental standards, large specimen
www.romantic-garden-nursery.co.uk

Suffolk Herbs Ltd.
Monks Farm
Coggeshall Road
Kelvedon
Essex CO5 9PG
Old European varieties of herbs, flowers and vegetables
www.suffolkherbs.co.uk

Sutton Seeds Ltd.
Hele Road
Torquay
Devon TQ2 7QJ
Sweet peas, flowers, fruit and vegetables
www.suttons-seeds.co.uk

Thompson & Morgan (Ipswich) Ltd.
Poplar Lane
Ipswich
Suffolk IP8 3BU
Flower seeds still used in Victorian bedding schemes in Sri Lanka, flowers, fruit and vegetables
www.thompson-morgan.com

Unwins Seeds Ltd.
Mail Order Department
Histon
Cambridgeshire CB4 4ZZ
Sweet peas, flower and vegetable seeds
www.unwins-seeds.co.uk

Unites States of America

Crystal Palace Perennials
12029 Wicker Avenue
Cedar Lake, IN 46303
Water plants
www.crystalpalaceperennial.com

Excelsa Gardens
12839 25th Street N
Loxahatchee, FL 33470
Exotic and novelty tropical plants
www.excelsagardens.com

Johnny's Selected Seeds
184, Foss Hill Road
Albion, ME 04910
Heirloom seeds
www.johnnyseeds.com

Klehm's Song Sparrow Perennial Farm
13101 East Rye Road
Avalon, WI 53505
Established over 150 years - trees, shrubs and perennials
www.songsparrow.com

The Park Seed Co.
1 Parkton Avenue
Greenwood, SC 29647-0001
Established 1868 - seeds, bulbs and plants
www.parkseed.com

Raintree Nursery
391, Butts Road
Morton, WA 98356
700+ fruit cultivars
www.raintreenursery.com

Rose Hill Garden
4955 Highway 955 West
Ethel, LA 70730
www.rosehillgarden.com

Seeds of Change
PO Box 15700
Santa Fe, NM 87506-5700
Heirloom and traditional seeds, garlic and potatoes
www.seedsofchange.com

Wayside Gardens
1 Garden Lane
Hodges, SC 29695-0001
Perennials, shrubs, vines and bulbs
www.waysidegardens.com

France

Etablissements Botaniques Latour-Marliac
47110 Le Temple sur Lot
Lot et Garonne

Selected Bibliography

Beeton, Samuel. *Beeton's New Dictionary of Everyday Gardening*. London, England: Ward, Lock & Co. c. 1896.

Brent, Elliott. Victorian Gardens. London: B.T. Batsford. 1986.

Burpee, W. Atlee & Company. *Burpee's Farm Annual - 1888*. Philadelphia PA: W. Atlee Burpee & Co. 1975 (Replica of 1888 catalog).

Carter, Tom. *The Victorian Garden*. London: Bracken Books. 1984.

Clayton-Payne, Andrew. *Victorian Flower Gardens*. London: Weidenfeld & Nicolson Ltd., 1994.

Downing, Andrew. *Cottage Residences*. 1842

Edwards, Paul and Katherine Swift. *Pergolas, Arbours and Arches: Their History and How to Make Them*. UK & USA: Barn Elms Publishing, 2001. (1899531068).

Hayden, Peter *Biddulph Grange, A Victorian Garden Rediscovered*. George Philip in association with The National Trust, 1989.

Hibberd, Shirley. *Rustic Adornments for Homes of Taste*. (1856) National Trust Classic, 1974.

Holmes, Caroline. *Icons of Garden Design*. Munich: Prestel Publishing, 2001.

Holmes, Caroline. *Monet at Giverny*. New York: Cassell. 2001.

Huxley, Anthony. *An Illustrated History of Gardening*. Paddington Press, 1978.

Jekyll, Gertrude. *Colour Schemes for the Flower Garden*. UK(1992 Antique Collectors Club 1-85149-216X) hardback; USA (1982 088143000-5) hardback

Jekyll, Gertrude. *Home and Garden*. UK & USA (1994 Antique Collectors Club 1-85149-196-1) paperback.

Jekyll, Gertrude & Lawrence Weaver. *Gardens for the Small Country House*. UK & USA (1980 Antique Collectors Club 0-90746210-3). Publisher out of stock; republished as: *The Arts and Crafts Garden*. UK(1996 Antique Collectors Club) & USA (1997 Dimensions 1870673166).

Loudon, Jane. *Ladies' Companion to the Flower Garden*. 1841.

Stearn, William T. Edited by John Lindley: *Gardener-Botanist and Pioneer Orchidologist*. Antique Collector's Club, 1999.

Stuart, David. *The Garden Triumphant*. New York: Harper & Row 1988.

Robinson, William. *The English Flower Garden*. UK (1998 Bloomsbury 0-74753833-6); USA(1995 Sagapress 0898310318).

Taylor, Geoffrey. *The Victorian Flower Garden*. Skeffington, 1952.

Thompson's The Gardener's Assistant 6 vols. The Gresham Publishing Company, 19thc.

The Fruit and Vegetable Finder compiled from the Heritage Seed Library of HDRA - the organic organisation and the National Fruit Collection at Brogdale Horticultural Trust.

Second hand Victorian gardening books can still be found relatively inexpensively; some are unreadable, others a superb insight into both the designs, maintenance, and varieties available.

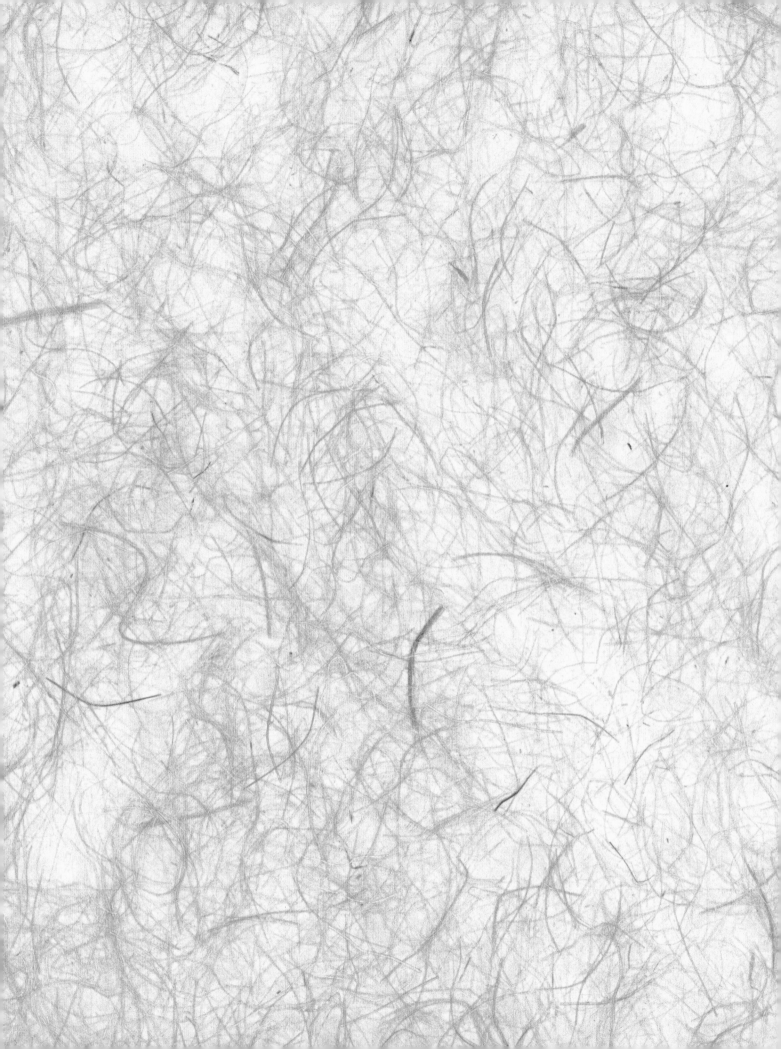